CULTURE AND
CUSTOMS OF JORDAN

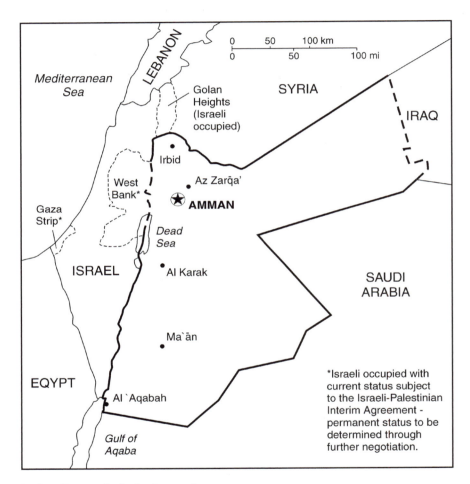

Jordan. Cartography by Bookcomp, Inc.

CULTURE AND CUSTOMS
OF JORDAN

John A. Shoup

Culture and Customs of the Middle East

Greenwood Press
Westport, Connecticut • London

Library of Congress Cataloging-in-Publication Data

Shoup, John A.
  Culture and customs of Jordan / John A. Shoup.
    p. cm. — (Culture and customs of the Middle East, ISSN 1550–1310)
  Includes bibliographical references and index.
  ISBN 0–313–33671–7 (alk. paper)
  1. Ethnology—Jordan.   2. Jordan—Social life and customs.   I. Title.
  GN635.J6S56   2006
  306.095695—dc22   2006029541

British Library Cataloguing in Publication Data is available.

Library of Congress Catalog Card Number: 2006029541
ISBN-10: 0–313–33671–7
ISBN-13: 978–0–313–33671–3
ISSN: 1550–1310

First published in 2007

Greenwood Press, 88 Post Road West, Westport, CT 06881
An imprint of Greenwood Publishing Group, Inc.
www.greenwood.com

Printed in the United States of America

The paper used in this book complies with the
Permanent Paper Standard issued by the National
Information Standards Organization (Z39.48–1984).

10 9 8 7 6 5 4 3 2 1

Contents

Series Foreword

At last! *Culture and Customs of the Middle East* fills a deep void in reference literature by providing substantial individual volumes on crucial countries in the explosive region. The series is available at a critical juncture, with, among other events, the recent war on Iraq, the continued wrangling by U.S. interests for control of regional oil resources, the quest for Palestinian independence, and the spread of religious fundamentalist violence and repression. The authoritative, objective, and engaging cultural overviews complement and balance the volley of news bites.

As with the other Culture and Customs series, the narrative focus is on contemporary culture and life, in a historical context. Each volume is written for students and general readers by a country expert. Contents include:

Chronology

Context, including land, people, and brief historical overview

Religion and world view

Literature

Media

Cinema

Art and architecture/housing

Cuisine and dress

Gender, marriage, and family

Social customs and lifestyle

Music and dance

Acknowledgments

Any work such as this always includes a large number of people who have helped one way or another. I would like to begin by thanking the Bedouin families who allowed me to live with them and to come back numerous times. I would like to especially express my gratitude to Muhammad Abu Shahir al-Faqir, his wife, 'Allal Umm Shahir, and their whole family for taking me in and making me one of them. I would also like to make special mention of Dakhl Allah Qublan and family, 'Ali Mutlaq and family, and Musa Huwaymil and family. I would also like to thank Elias Muqhar and his wife, Kay, Muhammad Fath Allah al-Bukhari and family, 'Abd al-Muhsin and Khalid Dughaythir for not only their help in the field but also for their generosity and willingness to share with me their knowledge of the region, its history, and culture. I would like to express my thanks to Dr. Philip Hammond who introduced me to the Bedouin in southern Jordan and for his constant encouragement. I want to thank Dr. Michael Fuller and his wife, Neathery Batsell Fuller, who allowed to assist in the ethnoarcheological work at 'Ayn Quwaylbah (Abilah), which gave me the chance to spend time in villages in northern Jordan. It would be remiss if I didn't express my thanks to Dr. Rebecca Torstrick who recommended my name to Greenwood Press. I want to mention both Wendi Schnaufer and Kaitlin Ciarmiello of Greenwood who have been such good working partners, though all via email. Finally, I want to thank my parents who have always encouraged all of us to do what we want to even if others thought I should get a "real" job.

Preface

Most people in Europe and North America are not very familiar with Jordan, a small country located between its larger, better known neighbors Egypt, Syria, Iraq, Israel/Palestine, and Saudi Arabia. If they do know something about it, it is often because of T. E. Lawrence, Lawrence of Arabia, whose exploits with the Bedouin during World War I have helped perpetuate the romantic images of robed Bedouin riding camels and dramatic desert landscapes. Others may be aware of Jordan because it has been a frontline Arab state in the long struggle between the Palestinians and Israelis. Still others may be aware of the country because it is mentioned in both the Old and New Testaments. In reality Jordan is all of these images; it is where a number of important battles did take place between the Bedouin forces of the Arab Revolt led by Lawrence as well as their tribal shaykhs and the Turks during World War I; it is one of the major frontline states with Israel starting even before Israel declared itself a state in 1948; and it does contain a large number of sites associated with both the Old and New Testaments, but it is much more.

Jordan was created out of the marginal areas of several older historical administrative districts after the collapse of the Ottoman Empire at the end of World War I. When its borders were drawn up in Cairo in 1920 and named the Emirate of the Transjordan, it was a poor, thinly populated country with settled agriculturalists hugging the better watered western spine and the rest was the home of nomadic pastoralists. Since gaining its full independence in 1946 the Hashemite Kingdom of Jordan has been able to create a strong sense of identity based on Bedouin culture among its people. It has emerged since the mid 1970s as a major business and banking center for the

Middle East with one of the best educated populations in the region, if not the world.

Proud of their Bedouin heritage, Jordanians are hospitable and generous. In fact, their hospitality is constantly evoked in the common greeting *ahlayn wa sahlayn*, "you are twice welcome." Jordanians use the phrase not only to say "hello," but also to say "you're welcome," "goodbye," and numerous other uses. Also frequently heard is *marhabtayn*, which again means "twice welcome." In fact, Jordan is called the Land of *Ahlan wa Sahlan*, the Land of Welcome, both by its own people and other Arabs in the Middle East. Jordan remains the Land of Welcome where traditional Arab hospitality is always given to the stranger with no questions asked as well as an island of peace and stability despite the conflicts the rend much of the region.

Chronology

NATUFIAN CULTURE

11,000–9,300 B.C. Proto-Neolithic—beginnings of permanent settlements between 10,000 and 9,000 B.C.—domestication of plants and animals.

NEOLITHIC PERIOD

8,350–4,000 B.C. Jericho one of the first places where wheat is known to have been domesticated.

8,300–4,500 B.C. Pre-Pottery Neolithic A and B major sites associated with the origin of agriculture are located in Jordan including those referred to as "mega-sites" of some 10 to 15 hectares in size.

7,520–4,000 B.C. 'Ayn Ghazal—a "mega-site" located near modern 'Amman—features include paved streets and a collection of clay statues of humans.

6,800–6,000 B.C. al-Baydhah—a "mega-site" located in southern Jordan—the site was abandoned when climate change made it hard to grow dry land crops of wheat and barley.

YARMUKIAN CULTURE

6,000–4,000 B.C. Climate change caused an economic change from dry land farming to raising livestock such as sheep and goats—wheat and barely restricted to the better rain-fed areas of the north and the river valleys.

CHALCOLITHIC PERIOD

4500–3100 B.C.   Use of copper and bronze tools as well as stone.

Bronze Age

3100–1200 B.C.   Concentration of settlements in the regions that would eventually give rise to local kingdoms Moab and Rabboth Ammon around 1300 B.C. while the rest of the south and east is abandoned to pastoral nomads who herd sheep and goats.

Iron Age

1200–539 B.C.   Kingdoms of Edom, Moab, Rabboth Ammon, and Gilead established.

Arrival of the Hebrews in the early Iron Age— begin series of wars with local kingdoms both in Transjordan and Cisjordan (Palestine) that will last until the Babylonians destroy Judah.

1025–1004 B.C.   Saul rules Kingdom of Israel—consolidates control on both sides of the Jordan River.

1004–965 B.C.   King David—wars with Raboth Ammon, Moab, and Edom.

1,000–612 B.C.   Assyrian Empire—numerous campaigns against the kingdoms of Syria, Jordan, and Palestine.

965–928 B.C.   King Soloman—height of power and control over the other kingdoms.

928 B.C.   Death of Soloman the Kingdom of Israel is divided into Israel in the north and Judah to the south— continued wars with the Transjordanian kingdoms.

840 B.C.   King Mesha of Moab defeats King Jeroham of Israel and gains independence according to the Mesha Stela found at Dibon.

853 B.C.   Battle of Qarqar Assyrian King Shalmaneser defeats the coalition of Aramean kingdoms and Arab chieftains from the Syrian Desert (including Jordan).

720 B.C.   Sargon II destroys the Kingdom of Israel.

612 B.C.   Babylonians conquer Assyria and take Nineveh the capital city.

605–539 B.C.   Babylonian domination and conquests of Syria, Lebanon, Jordan, and Palestine.

588 B.C.	Nebuchadnezzar destroys Kingdom of Judah.

Persian Period

539–333 B.C.	Arrival of the Nabateans in the late 7th early 6th century B.C. push the Edomites into Palestine where they are called Idumeans.
539 B.C.	the Persian King Cyrus the Great conquers the area and divides it into 23 administrative districts under Persian Satraps or Governors—allows the exiled Jews to return to Palestine and rebuild Jerusalem.
333 B.C.	Alexander the Great conquers the Persian Empire.

Hellenistic Period 333–64 B.C

323 B.C.	Alexander dies in Babylon and his empire is divided among his generals.
312 B.C.	Antigonus I Monophtalmus Greek ruler of Syria attempts to plunder the Nabatean capital "Petra" (in Greek) but is defeated by the Nabateans.
311 B.C.	Seleucus I Nicator begins Seleucid Dynasty—originally given area of Mesopotamia as his share of Alexander's empire.
301 B.C.	Seleucus I Nicator defeats Antigonus I and Syria is joined to Mesopotamia—some 50,000 Greek soldiers are settled in the region to Hellenize the culture—soldiers are settled in both older existing cities and newly founded Greek colonies called the "Ten Cities" or the Decapolis most of which are in Jordan.
Second century B.C.	the Nabateans are firmly established with Petra as their capital city—they dominate the trade between southern Arabia and the Mediterranean.
	King Aretas III (86–62 B.C.) expands the Nabatean Kingdom and occupies Damascus in 85 B.C.

Roman Period 64 B.C.–395 A.D.

64 B.C.	Rome imposes peace on the warring states of the eastern Mediterranean making them all subject to Roman control though leaving them with their local governments.

	Period of the greatest Nabatean King, Aretas IV (9 B.C. to 40 A.D.)—height of Nabatean power and wealth.
106 A.D.	The Roman Emperor Trajan annexes the Nabatean Kingdom as the Province Arabia Petrea.
Second and third centuries A.D.	Roman limes or series of forts built to protect the eastern frontier and keep Arab Bedouin tribes out of Roman territory—rebuilt in fourth and fifth centuries—by the sixth century they are manned by local Arab troops, for example al-Qastal seems to have been built by the Ghassanid Harith ibn Jabala (531–571).
313 A.D.	Emperor Constantine gives official recognition to the Christian church and encourages it as the state religion.

Byzantine Period

395–636 A.D.	Growing divisions between Christian communities over the nature of Christ split the church into numerous smaller divisions—the Byzantine Emperor interferes and gives support to specific interpretations forcing the others to abide by state-church council decisions.
	Jordan produces a flowering of early Byzantine culture especially in church mosaics—for example at Madaba, Mount Nebo, Jerash, Umm Risas, and Petra.
	Movement of the trade routes north to Palmyra (Tadmur) in the third century, several severe earthquakes in the fourth to sixth centuries A.D., and the growing tension and war between Rome/Byzantium and Persia causes the economy of the region to decline.
	Bedouin Arab tribes allowed inside Byzantine territory establish themselves in Jordan, Syria, and Iraq.
Early fourth century A.D.	The Bani Ghassan tribe arrives in Syria become a vassal state to the Byzantines and aid them in their wars with the Persians.
529	The Ghassanid leader Harith ibn Jabala is appointed Phylarch by the Emperor Justinian.
541	Harith leads the Arab units in the army under the Byzantine general Belisarius during his Mesopotamian campaign.

554	Harith defeats and kills the Lakhmid Arab king Mundhir allied to the Persians.
572	Harith's son Mundhir defeats the Lakhmid king Qabus ibn al-Hind.
580	Mundhir ibn Harith is crowned "King of the Arabs" by the Byzantine Emperor Tiberias.
611–629	Devastating war between Byzantium and Persia ends in Persian defeat after a long Persian occupation of Syria, Lebanon, Jordan, and Palestine.
629	The Ghassanid Jabala ibn Ayham appointed "King of the Arabs" by the Byzantine Emperor Heraclius.
629–630	The Prophet Muhammad leads an expedition to the northern Hijaz and established treaties with the Christian leader of al-'Aqabah and the Jewish leaders of Maqna, Udhrah, and al-Jarba in southern Jordan. In addition the Bedouin tribes of Bani Udhra and Billi submitted to Islam. The Muslim commander Khalid ibn al-Walid captured the oasis of Jauf from the Ghassanids and its governor converts to Islam.
632	The Prophet Muhammad dies and Abu Bakr is elected *Khalifah* (Caliph) or Successor to the Prophet.

The Rightly Guided *Khalifah*s—632–661 A.D.

629	Muslim forces first penetrate into Jordan.
633	*Khalifah* Abu Bakr consolidated the Muslim state defeating rebellious tribes.
634	Battle of Ajnadayn in Palestine Byzantine forces defeated.
634	Abu Bakr dies and is succeeded by Umar ibn al-Khattab as *Khalifah*.
635	Damascus surrenders to the Arabs for the first time.
636	Battle of Yarmuk—the Muslims defeat the Byzantines and their Bani Ghassan vassals taking control of all of Jordan, Palestine, Syria, and Lebanon as a result.
636	Damascus surrenders for the second and final time to the Arabs.

637   Umar ibn al-Khattab divided the newly conquered
                area into four military districts: Palestine (*Filistin*),
                Jordan (*al-Urdunn*), Damascus (*Dimashq*), and
                Homs (*Hims*).

639   Year of Ashes—Syria and northern Hijaz are
                devastated by famine and plague. Among the victims
                were many of the Companions of the Prophet
                Muhammad—Mu'awiyah ibn Abi Sufyan becomes
                governor of Syria. The *Khalifah* 'Umar ibn al-Khat-
                tab makes of tour of Syria.

644   'Umar is assassinated and 'Uthman ibn 'Affan is
                elected *Khalifah*.

656   'Uthman is assassinated and Ali ibn Abi Talib
                is elected. Mu'awiyah refuses to agree to 'Ali as
                Khalifah and accuses 'Ali of being party to 'Uthman's
                assassination.

657   Battle of Siffin ends with both sides agreeing to
                mediation.

658   Both parties meet at Dumat al-Jandal but no
                agreement is reached. 'Ali remains *Khalifah* until his
                assassination in 660. Mu'awiyah begins to use the
                title *Khalifah* in 660.

Umayyad Period 661–750 A.D.

661   Mu'awiyyah bin Abi Sufyan establishes the Umayyad
                Dynasty with Damascus as the capital.

                Desert Castles of Qusayr 'Amra, Hallabat, Qasr
                Kharanah, Hammam al-Sarakh, Qasr Tuba, and
                Mushatta—The Umayyads build numerous pleasure
                and hunting lodges in the Jordanian desert—helped
                to maintain close ties with the Bedouin tribes in the
                Syrian desert—Umayyad princes sent to the desert to
                learn "proper Arabic"—frequent marriages between
                Umayyad princes and daughters of Bedouin *shaykh*s.

'Abbasid Period 750–968 A.D.

750–754   al-Saffah—first 'Abbasid *Khalifah*—orders the death
                of all members of the Umayyad family.

750	'Abbasid Revolution removes the Umayyad Dynasty—shift in the seat of government from Syria to Iraq.
754–775	al-Mansur *Khalifah.*
762	Baghdad founded as the new capital.
813	Damascus rebels against the 'Abbasids.
842	New revolts in Syria—spread of Shi'ism.
902	Qaramitah activities in the Syrian desert convert Bedouin tribes to Isma'ili Shi'ism.
906–907	Qaramitah revolt in Syria.
964	Qaramitah attack on Palestine defeats the Ikhshidids ruling southern Syria and Egypt in the name of the 'Abbasids.
969	Fatimids take Egypt from the Ikhshidids and the Qaramitah defeat the Ikhsidids in Palestine

Fatimid Period 969–1055 A.D.

969	Fatimids conquer Egypt and found Cairo (*al-Qahirah*).
948–1076	Fatimids control southern Syria including Jordan and Palestine.

Seljuq Period 1055–1128 A.D.

1055	Seljuqs take northern Syria for the 'Abbasids ending decades of autonomous local Arab dynasties.
1070–1072	Alp Arlsan *Sultan.*
1071	Battle of Manzikert the Seljuqs defeat the Byzantines and open up Anatolia to Turkish settlement—secure control over all of Syria including briefly Palestine and Jordan.
1072–1092	Malik Shah Seljuq *Sultan.*
1095	Pope Urban II preaches holy Crusade against the Seljuqs.
1099	Jerusalem taken by the First Crusade—a large number of Muslims seek refuge in Damascus founding several of the city's quarters.

1115	Crusader Kingdom of Jerusalem builds castle called Montreal at Showbak in southern Jordan to raid Muslim caravans going between Syria, the Hijaz, and Egypt—other forts and castles were built or rebuilt in southern Jordan and on the Island of Graye or Jazirat Far'un in the Gulf of 'Aqabah.
1116–1154	Turkish military commander Tughtagin rules Damascus and most of Jordan for the Fatamids of Egypt.
1119	Battle of Sarmada first major defeat for the Crusaders by the Seljuqs of Aleppo.
1124–1125	Crusaders try to take Aleppo but fail.

Zengid Period 1128–1174 A.D.

1128–1146	Atabek 'Imad al-Din al-Zengi regent of Aleppo in northern Syria—begins counter-crusade.
1142	Crusaders build a castle called Pierre du Désert at Kerak, which was one of the most important in the Transjordan-made seat of the Barony of Oultre-Jourdain.
1144	'Imad al-Din al-Zengi takes Edessa from the Crusaders.
1146–1174	Nur al-Din Mahmud al-Zengi rules most of Syria.
1147–1149	Second Crusade attempts to take Damascus and is defeated by Nur al-Din.
1154	Nur al-Din returns to Damascus at the invitation of its people and includes southern Syria (including parts of northern and eastern Jordan) in his state.
1163	Nur al-Din interferes in Fatamid Egypt on behalf of the deposed Wazir or Chief Minister Shawar.
1164	Nur al-Din restores Shawar but the rival Wazir seeks help from Amalric the Latin King of Jerusalem.
1167–1169	Nur al-Din and Amalric support opposite sides in the power struggle in Egypt—Nur al-Din emerges victor and his military commander, Salah al-Din al-Ayyubi, is appointed the Wazir by the Fatamid *Khalifah*, which, in effect, combines Egypt with Syria under Nur al-Din's rule.
1171	al-'Adid last Fatamid *Khalifah* dies leaving Salah al-Din ruler of Egypt.

| 1174 | Nur al-Din dies and his 11 year old son Isma'il ruler. |
| 1176 | Salah al-Din unifies Syria and Egypt. |

Ayyubid Period 1176–1260 A.D.

1176–1193	Salah al-Din al-Ayyubi rules Syria and Egypt.
1183	Salah al-Din orders 'Izz al-Din Usamah to build the fort Qasr or Qala'at al-Rabbadh at Jabal 'Ajlun to threaten Latin held Jordan.
1183	Attempted sea attack on Makkah by Renaud de Châtillon Lord of Kerak ends in defeat.
1187	Renaud de Châtillon breaks the truce with Salah al-Din and provokes war.
1187	Battle of Hattin Crusaders defeated- Jerusalem returned to Muslim rule.
1188	Kerak falls to Salah al-Din.
1189	Showbak falls to Salah al-Din—ends Latin occupation of the Transjordan.
1187–1192	Third Crusade—ends with Crusaders in control of some coastal cities—Jerusalem remains in Muslim hands.
1193	Salah al-Din dies and kingdom is divided among members of the family—dynastic disputes weaken the Ayyubids.
1217–1221	Fifth Crusade ends in failure.
1249	al-Malik al-Salih Najm al-Din dies—his wife Shajarat al-Durr becomes ruler of Egypt.
1250–1259	quick succession of three Mamluk *Sultan*s.
1258–1260	Mongol invasion under Hulegu Khan—Baghdad sacked and the 'Abbasid *Khalifah* al-Musta'sim is executed.

Mamluk Period 1260–1516 A.D.

1260	Battle of 'Ayn Jalut in Palestine the Mamluks defeat the Mongols.
1260–1382	Period of the Bahri Mamluks of mainly Turkish and Mongol origin.
1260–1277	al-Zahir Baybars *Sultan* and Kerak in Jordan becomes one of his "capitals" along with Cairo and Damascus.

1382–1516	Period of the Burji Mamluks of mainly Circassian origin.

Ottoman Period 1516–1918 A.D.

1516	Battle of Marj Dabiq the Ottomans are victorious and take the Mamluk provinces in Syria and Arabia including the area of present day Jordan.
1867	Ottomans reimpose control over the Transjordan.
1878	Ottoman government begins settling Circassian and Shishans from the Caucasus Mountains in Jordan.
1900	Construction on the Hejaz Railway linking Damascus with Madinah begins.
1906	Hejaz Railway reaches 'Amman.
1916–1918	The Arab Revolt—Sharif Husein Hussein of Makkah with British backing declares independence from the Ottomans and his sons Faysal, 'Abdallah, and 'Ali command the military.
1918	The Arab Army under Faysal and T. E. Lawrence (Lawrence of Arabia) takes Damascus from the Ottomans.

Modern Period 1918 A.D. to present

1920	Faysal declared King of Syria by the Syrian National Congress.
	Treaty of San Remo establishes the mandate system—Iraq, Palestine, and Transjordan are declared British while Lebanon and Syria are French.
	Battle of Maysalun French troops defeat King Faysal's army and impose French Mandate over Syria.
	'Abdallah arrives in southern Jordan to support his brother King Faisal in Syria.
1921	British recognize 'Abdallah as *Amir* of the Transjordan.
	British install Faysal as King of Iraq.
1936–1939	Palestinian Revolt.
1945	Arab League established with Jordan as a founding member.
1946	Hashemite Kingdom of Jordan proclaimed with Amir 'Abdallah becoming King 'Abdallah.

1948–1949	First war with Israel—Jordanian army defends the West Bank and East Jerusalem.
1950	Act of Unification of the Palestinian West Bank to Jordan.
1951	King 'Abdallah assassinated in Jerusalem and Prince Talal proclaimed king.
1952	King Talal abdicates.
1953	Hussein formally becomes King.
1956	Suez Crisis—Egyptian President Gamal Abd al-Nasser nationalizes the Suez Canal—Britain, France, and Israel attack Egypt—U.S. and USSR force them to negotiate—President Nasser is seen in the Arab world as the champion of Arab nationalism.
1956–1958	Growth of Arab Nationalist—pro-Nasser sentiments in the government and among the people of Jordan.
1958–1961	Egypt and Syria form the short lived United Arab Republic and Jordan and Iraq form the Arab Federation.
1958	Revolution in Iraq ends Hashemite rule and breaks the Arab Federation of Jordan and Iraq.
1964	First Arab Summit creates the Palestine Liberation Organization.
1966	Israeli raid into Jordanian territory pushes King Hussein into closer relations with Egypt and Syria.
1967	Jordan signs the Joint Defense Agreement with Egypt.
	June or Six Day War Israel defeats the Arab armies and seizes the West Bank, Golan Heights, and Sinai.
1968	Israeli army pushes into the Jordanian side of the Jordan River and is defeated by combined Palestinian and Jordanian forces at Battle of Karamah.
1970	Popular Front for the Liberation of Palestine hijack a number of international airlines that precipitate the clash between the Jordanian army and Palestinian fighters.
	Black September the Jordanian army defeats Palestinian fighters and begin their expulsion from Jordan.

1971	Jordanian army forces last of the armed Palestinians out of the country and most find refuge in Lebanon.
1973	October War—Jordan does not participate directly.
1974	Arab League meeting the Palestine Liberation Organization recognized as the legitimate representative of the Palestinian people instead of Jordan.
1976	King Hussein meets with Yasir 'Arafat and begins the post-Rabat thaw in relations.
1978	September, Camp David Agreement signed—November, Arab Summit in Baghdad pledges massive economic assistance for Jordan's steadfastness.
1982	Israel invades Lebanon.
1984	Palestine National Council meets in 'Amman.
1985	Jordan and the Palestinians agree on coordination in the peace process.
1987	First Palestinian *Intifadah* begins.
1988	Jordan withdraws all administrative and legal ties with the West Bank.
1989	Jordan begins implementation of the IMF program for readjustment of its economy—Riots in Ma'an—first free and fair elections held and the Islamists win.
1990	Iraq invades Kuwait—King Hussein tries to be a mediator.
1991	Jordan participates in the Madrid Arab-Israeli summit.
1993	Jordan holds first multi-party election since 1956.
1994	Jordan and Israel sign a formal peace treaty.
1999	January King Hussein changes succession from his brother Hasan to his son 'Abdallah—February King Hussein dies, 'Abdallah becomes 'Abdallah II and Hamzah is declared Crown Prince.
2000	Second Palestinian *Intifadah* begins.
2003	United States invades Iraq to force a regime change—continued unrest in Iraq creates an unstable environment for Jordan and Saudi Arabia—al-Qa'idah's Jordanian-born operative Abu Mus'ab al-Zarqawi linked to numerous insurgent actions in Iraq.

2005   U.S. military ships docked at al-'Aqabah are fired upon by al-Qa'idah operatives killing one Jordanian soldier. In November Jordan has its own 9/11 as suicide bombers linked to Abu Mus'ab's group in Iraq attack three hotels in 'Amman, killing 56 people (of which 33 are Jordanians attending wedding parties). Among the dead is the Syrian-American film director Mustapha Akkad.

2006   Gunman shoots six tourists, killing one and wounding the others, at the Roman Amphitheater in downtown 'Amman. Though no motive is known, it seems to be connected to the ongoing war in Iraq and the Israeli war with Hizballah in southern Lebanon.

1

Land, People, and History of Jordan

Jordan is a country that is both old and new. The Hashemite Kingdom of Jordan dates to only 1946 when the Emirate of the Transjordan became independent; however, the Kingdom includes some of the oldest sites where humans first settled into permanent villages. The present borders of the Kingdom were carved out of former provinces of the Ottoman Turkish Empire and throughout most of its history, Jordan has been tied closely to its neighbors: Palestine, Syria, Arabia, and to a lesser degree Iraq and Egypt. Culturally Jordanians have long shared a good deal with Palestinians and Syrians and the creation of the modern states in the region in the early twentieth century has cut across historical connections.

Jordan is part of the Mediterranean even if it has no borders on the Mediterranean Sea. 'Amman, the capital, is located only 75 miles (112 kilometers) from the sea, and on a clear, sunny day it is possible to see the sun's reflection off of the golden dome of the Dome of the Rock Mosque in Jerusalem, only 40 miles (60 kilometers) away. Breezes from the Mediterranean cool the 'Ajlun highlands in the summer and bring needed moisture in the winter. Like all Mediterranean countries, Jordan has hot, dry summers and cold, wet winters.

GEOGRAPHY

The geography and environment of Jordan have been major factors in the settlement patterns and economic systems throughout its history. The availability or lack of water supply has been and remains today the single most important environmental factor, and some 80 percent of the country is desert receiving less than 5 inches (150 millimeters) of rain a year. There are few permanent rivers that are found in the northern highlands and, in addition, there are a number of seasonal streams throughout the country that usually run with water only after a rainstorm. Most of these streams flow into the Rift Valley while a few run east into the Syrian Desert or Badiyat al-Sham where they die.

Though the borders of the Kingdom Jordan were drawn by politicians at a conference in Cairo following the World War I, they do, to a degree, correspond to some of the important physical features. Part of the northern border with Syria follows the short course of the Yarmuk River, the western border is defined by the Rift Valley, and the south is formed by the Gulf of 'Aqabah and the steep mountains of the Hijaz. Part of Jordan's eastern border with Saudi Arabia is defined by the Wadi Sirhan, the second largest valley system in Jordan.

The most dominant physical feature in Jordan is the Rift Valley system, which begins near Ma'arsh in southern Turkey, runs through Syria and the entire length of Jordan's western border, forms the Gulf of 'Aqabah, the Red Sea, and the Lake Region of East Africa, and eventually runs back out into the Indian Ocean for a total length of 3,100 miles (5,000 kilometers). In Jordan most of the Rift system forms the Jordan River valley, the Dead Sea, and Wadi 'Arabah. Much of the Jordan Valley is below sea level, with its lowest point (the bottom of the Dead Sea) being 2,642 feet (800 meters) below sea level. The Rift Valley in Jordan is not wide, averaging only 10 miles (25 kilometers) in width. The whole system remains active and there are small earthquakes on nearly a daily basis. Major earthquakes in the past were responsible for the eventually abandonment of several ancient sites such as Petra in the sixth century A.D.

The Jordan River has a number of major tributary streams that flow into it from the east. The most important of these are the Yarmuk (shared with Syria) and the Zarqa'. The Yarmuk begins in Jabal Druze in southern Syria and runs for a total length of only 40 kilometers (slightly longer than 26 miles), but is an important tributary of the Jordan and source for irrigated agriculture for both Syria and Jordan. Its narrow but deep valley serves as a natural border separating the Golan (Jawlan) in Syria from Jabal 'Ajlun in Jordan. The Zarqa' is also a short river starting just to the north of 'Amman and forms the southern limit of the 'Ajlun district as it flows westward into the Jordan River. A third river, the Shu'ayb, has been so heavily used for irrigated agriculture for so long that it stopped flowing in the 1970s. The Zarqa' and the Yarmuk are also heavily used for irrigated agriculture and have very little water in them most of the year. In addition to the few permanent streams, there are a number of seasonal ones, most of which flow into the Jordan River or directly into the Dead Sea. These include Wadi Mujib, Wadi Hasa, and Wadi Zarqa' Ma' 'Ayn, whose steep valleys helped form the borders of the ancient kingdoms of Rabboth Ammon, Moab, and Edom.

Wadi Sirhan is another Rift-like valley, though not as deep or as dramatic as the main Rift complex. Wadi Sirhan flows to the east and what little water there is drains into Saudi Arabia during the wet, winter season. The Wadi is dotted with wells serving as important watering places for the herds and flocks of nomadic Bedouin and for irrigation for the few villages located there. To the northwest of Wadi Sirhan is an important oasis of natural pools and small lakes called Azraq (Blue in Arabic). The fresh water pools attract a wide range of wildlife, especially migratory birds, as well as herds belonging to pastoral nomads. The Jordanian government established the Shawmari Wildlife Refuge in the Azraq and organized an integrated usage pattern between Bedouin-owned herds and rare wildlife, some of them reintroduced into the wild in the 1970s. However, since the 1980s Azraq's water has been tapped to help supply the growing demand for drinking water in 'Amman and the result is that many of the pools are now dry.

The eastern side of the Rift system in Jordan consists of a series of highlands; in the north they are called Jabal 'Ajlun, in the central area they are called Jabal al-Balqa, and in the south they are called Jabal al-Sharat or Bilad al-Sharat. These mountains are rough and broken with steep, deep valleys carved by both permanent and seasonal streams. The highlands are tall enough for some winter moisture to fall as snow, even in the southern Jabal al-Sharat. The peaks range in elevation from 3,000 to 4,000 feet (1,000 to 1,300 meters) in the north to more than 5,400 feet (1,800 meters) in the south. While the western slopes are steep and difficult to climb, the eastern sides gently slope down to the steppe and desert regions.

Rainfall, or the lack of it, is an important factor determining settlement patterns throughout the history of Jordan. As a whole, the country receives little rain with most of it concentrated in the northern highlands. Rain falls mainly in the winter season with little to no rain recorded in the months of May to November. Most of Jordan, some four-fifths of the country, receives no more than 5 inches (150 millimeters) a year. The lack of rainfall has had a major impact on the settlement patterns of the people with the majority concentrated in the north and on the spine of highlands along the Rift system where more rain falls. Moving further east and south the amount of rainfall drops rapidly from 25 inches (500 millimeters) a year in Jabal 'Ajlun to 1/2 an inch (less than 50 millimeters) a year at al-Mudawwarah near the southeastern border with Saudi Arabia.

CITIES, TOWNS, VILLAGES, AND TENTS

79 percent of Jordan's 5.7 million people live in the urban communities of 'Amman, al-Zarqa', Irbid, al-Salt, Karak, and the southern port city of al-'Aqabah. While officially the population of 'Amman is placed at 1.1 million people, if the greater 'Amman area (from al-Zarqa' and Suwaylah in the north to Yaduda in the south and west to Wadi al-Sir) is included nearly one-half of Jordan's people live there. 'Amman has grown at a rapid pace since it became the capital in 1921, but especially after the first Arab-Israeli War in 1948 when it received a large number of Palestinian refugees. Whole neighborhoods in 'Amman are actually Palestinian refugee camps. 'Amman had another growth after the 1967 War and again after 1975 as a result of the Lebanese Civil War when a number of banks and other businesses relocated there from Beirut.

Other important urban centers include Irbid, al-Salt, Karak, and al'-Aqabah. Many of these are ancient cities with origins stretching back into the Neolithic. Some of these smaller urban centers, such as Irbid, have also received numbers of Palestinian refugees. Several of these smaller cities and towns, such as Jarash, Tafilah, Dhiban, and Madaba, serve as important centers for agricultural marketing.

Jordan has a large number of villages, and like the cities and towns, some date back to the origins of settled life. The villages are the backbone of Jordan's agricultural sector, which is still one of the major sources of income. The distinction between village, town, and city is becoming more and more blurred as urban centers like 'Amman and Irbid expand into communities that were once their own separate entity.

Villages make up the majority of Jordan's rural population, which constitutes only 21 percent of the total population. The northern Jabal 'Ajlun region is densely populated with villages while in the south and east the numbers become far fewer. As noted above, some 80 percent of the country is desert. The Bedouin who live in the desert are nomadic pastoralists and pastoral products are important to the rural economy. Pastoral products such as milk, cheese, yogurt, meat, wool, hair, and leather are sold in towns and cities, and many Jordanians still prefer the taste of local meat and milk products over those imported from Europe or Australia.

PEOPLES

Modern Jordan is an Arab country with Arabs making up the vast majority of its people. Arabs began settling in Jordan during antiquity, something attested to in inscriptions by the Assyrians, Babylonians, and even in the Old Testament. The strong Arab element in the ancient population of Jordan is attested to in the names of such tribal peoples as the Kedarites (in the Old

Testament) and the names of tributary or rebellious "kings" and "queens" such as Jindibu the Arab, who joined the rebellion against the Assyrian Shalmaneser III (858–824 B.C.), and Samsi or Shamsi who was Queen of the Taymah Oasis at the time of Sargon II (721–705 B.C.). The Old Testament's story of Job is thought to be set in southern Jordan, and Job (Ayyub) is an Arab name. During the later periods of antiquity the Arabic speaking Nabateans established their kingdom in Jordan and just prior to the rise of Islam, the Arab Bani Ghassan established a kingdom as a vassal state to the Byzantine Emperor. Some of the Christian families from in and around Karak claim direct descent from the Bani Ghassan.

The Islamic conquest of Jordan, Palestine, and Syria in the seventh century A.D. allowed the movement of Bedouin tribes from the Arabian Peninsula into the region. The Umayyad dynasty (660–750 A.D.) encouraged tribes to whom they had blood connections through marriage to use the pastures in the Syrian Desert, pushing those already there deeper into Syria, Lebanon, and Palestine. At various times the population of Jordan would receive new waves of Bedouin tribes from the Peninsula looking for better water and pasture for their livestock. The last of these major movements occurred in the eighteenth century, establishing the current Bedouin populations in Syria and Jordan. While much of the population is of village or urban backgrounds, the Bedouin have set their seal firmly on Jordanian identity. The strong Bedouin character is evidenced in the spoken dialect of most Jordanians and sets them off from those of Palestinian origin.

BADU: BEDOUIN TRIBES OF JORDAN

Bedouin make up only between 7 percent to 10 percent of the overall Jordanian population today and even less if strictly defining Bedouin as those who raise livestock as their major source of income. Many Bedouin today are Bedouin only in the dialect they speak or in their family relations but have little or no direct connection to a pastoral nomadic lifestyle. While small in numbers, Bedouin have politically and culturally dominated the Syrian Desert for generations.

Bedouin are tribal, meaning that their social-political organization is based on the concept of tribe. The tribal system is one of ever larger numbers of people included as "family" members from the smallest unit of household to the largest unit of the entire tribe. Tribal leaders have limited authority and lead by example and persuasion rather than force, something states have had serious problems dealing with for centuries. Tribal leaders are elected by the general membership and can be quickly replaced should the people become unhappy with them.

Bedouin divide themselves into three major groups based on the type of pastoralism they practice and the livestock they keep. These divisions are: the *asil* (or noble/great tribes) who raise camels and range widely for pasture; the *shawayah* (or small/lesser tribes) who raise sheep and goats, which require a short range of pasture and need to remain near water; and the *ru'a* (or herders) who also have sheep and goats, but who also may live part or all of the year in permanent villages. The *asil* tribes have dominated the other Bedouin and settled peoples through a system called *khawah* or brotherhood tax. *Khawah* establishes a bond between the *asil* tribes to provide protection for smaller, less powerful tribes and settled villagers in exchange for goods, services, or money.

The most important *asil* Bedouin tribes in Jordan are the Ruwallah, Sirhan, Bani Khalid, Bani Hassan, 'Adwan, Bani Sakhr, Bani 'Atiyya, Hijaya, and Huwaytat. These tribes and their allies have played an important role in modern history of the region. Several of them have traditional pasture lands that take them beyond the borders of Jordan into Syria, Iraq, Saudi Arabia, Palestine, and even Egypt. All of these tribes are considered to be *asil* or noble, traditionally raising camels and if owning agricultural fields, they did not work the fields themselves.

The *shawayah* tribes, though perhaps not as famous as the *asil* tribes, constitute a large number of those who call themselves Bedouin. Restricted by the need to water their flocks of sheep and goats at least once a day, they have limited ranges and are not found in the deeper desert regions except during the wet, winter months. The *shawayah* are distinguished from the *ru'a* by the fact that they live a nomadic existence all the year, and until recently did not live in villages. Since the 1950s more and more of the *shawayah* have been settled in special Bedouin settlements built for them by the Jordanian government or have on their own moved to urban centers such as 'Amman, Irbid, Karak, or Ma'an. In the past the *shawayah* often took care of the small stock that belonged to Bedouin from *asil* tribes or even those that belonged to urban families.

The *ru'a*, or herders, are the third division of Bedouin and the term refers to those who live at least part of the year in permanent settlements, though this does not have to mean villages. The Bidul tribe of Petra, for example, lives scattered among the Nabatean tombs. However, defined communities often correspond to the camping units that herders live in over the summer. The Bidul do not pay their *shawayah* and *asil* neighbors *khawah* and are held to be "allies" of *hilf* by the powerful *asil* Huwaytat and as well as by the *shawayah* 'Ammarin. Like the *shawayah* tribes, the *ru'a* depend on small stock—sheep and goats—but also plant fields of wheat and barely as well as small gardens and orchards of olive, almonds, and pomegranates. Today the distinction between Bedouin is more historical as economic conditions for pastoralists have encouraged raising small stock such as sheep and more and more *asil* Bedouin are no longer keeping herds of camels.

In addition to the "Jordanian" Bedouin tribes, there are also Bedouin families displaced from Palestine who have tried to maintain a nomadic existence. They are usually called "Saba'win" from Bi'r al-Saba' (Beersheva) in the Negev Desert in southern Palestine. They are found throughout Jordan living in and among the Jordanian tribes. In southern Jordan, where many have close blood ties with Jordanian tribes, it is not easy to identify them unless their women still wear their distinctive face veils and embroidered dresses that separate them from the Jordanian Bedouin women.

SETTLED POPULATIONS OR HADAR

The majority of Jordan's population was and is composed of settled peoples, those who live year round in permanent settlements. Social and political organization for nearly all Jordanians favored tribalism and thus nearly all Jordanians of village origin are part of tribal confederations that arose in the period of loose Ottoman rule (late-1500s to mid-1800s). Villagers were left with no protection from raids by Bedouin and formed "tribal" entities to better defend themselves. The result has been a "Bedouinization" of the Jordanian population with many even taking on the speech, mannerisms, customs, and behavior of the Bedouin.

Palestinians make up a significant part of the Jordan's population, perhaps more than one-half. 'Amman, Irbid, al-Zarqa', Jarash, and other cities and towns have sizable Palestinian populations. There has been a long historical connection between the peoples living on both sides of the Jordan River going back into ancient times. Several Jordanian and Palestinian towns have "sister" connections with members of the same families living in both and with long held business partnerships; for example Karak with Hebron and al-Salt with Nablus.

The Palestinian Jordanians began arriving in numbers in the 1860s after the Ottomans reasserted their control over Jabal 'Ajlun. Around the same time the *shaykh*s of the Bedouin Bani Sakhr tribe established large farms south of the 'Amman and needed farm labor. Their own tribesmen would not work as farm laborers, therefore Palestinian peasants were brought in to farm for them. The numbers of Palestinians increased as a result of the growing frictions between Arab Palestinians and Jews following World War I that finally erupted into the Palestinian Revolt of 1936 to 1939. Other waves of Palestinians came as a result of the hostilities and wars between Israel and its Arab neighbors in 1948 and 1967. Palestinians were often better educated and skilled than their Jordanian neighbors and quickly formed an important professional class of educators, lawyers, civil servants, and doctors.

Non Arab Minorities

The Arab character of Jordan's people has been maintained even though non-Arabs have settled there. Other ethnic groups living in Jordan include the Armenians, Circassians, Shishans, and Turks. With the notable exception of the Christian Armenians, these groups are Sunni Muslims similar to the majority of the Arabs living around them.

The single largest non-Arab minority in Jordan is the Circassians and related Shishans (Chechens). Both the Circassians and Shishans came seeking the protection of the Ottoman Sultan in a number of waves starting soon after their region of the Caucasus Mountains was conquered by the Russians in 1859. Their arrival coincided with the resurgence of Ottoman control over the more remote, fringe areas of the empire, such as the Syrian Desert. With government assistance, Circassians and Shishans were settled in villages and towns in Syria, Palestine, and Jordan, such as Jarash, al-Zarqa', Wadi al-Sir, Na'ur, and Suwaylih. The towns formed very important points of stability and control in areas once under Bedouin domination. Some towns still have a majority of Circassians or Shishans, such as Wadi al-Sir and Jarash, and local building styles reflect the architecture of their Caucasus homelands.

Both Circassians and Shishans have "Arabized" within a short period of time adopting Arabic as their main language for public use. Their own languages were reserved for use at home, but even there, many began using Arabic instead of their own languages. In response to the heavy assimilation into the mainstream Arab culture, a Circassian and Shishan cultural revival began in the late 1980s in order to record and preserve their unique heritage.

Jordan's Turkish minority is composed of several different peoples who arrived at different times in history. The few Turkomans who have not been fully absorbed into the Arabs came as early as the Mamluk period and into the early part of the Ottoman period. Once nomadic pastoralists similar to the Arab Bedouin, most are now urban. Some Turkomans were settled in Jordan by the Ottomans at the same time as the Circassians and Shishans and served the same purpose to control areas once under Bedouin tribal authority. Turkish-speaking Uzbeks arrived after the Soviets took control of Central Asia in 1918. Persecution of Islamic scholars and religious figures caused a number of them to flee Russia and many eventually settled in Saudi Arabia and Jordan. In Jordan most Uzbeks live in 'Amman where they established a market called Suq al-Bukhariyyah, the Bukhari Market. Uzbeki Turkish remains the language of the home though it is losing ground to Arabic with each generation.

Most of the Armenians in Jordan came seeking refuge in the aftermath of the 1915 massacres in Anatolia. Armenians were accused of assisting the Russians who were the enemies of the Turkish state, acting as a fifth column behind Turkish lines. An estimated one million died at the hands of angry mobs or due to starvation and exposure after being evicted from their homes. Those Armenians able to escape the slaughter in eastern Anatolia found refuge in Syria, Lebanon, Jordan, Palestine, and Egypt. The Armenians are Christians belonging to one of the oldest established churches in the world, the Armenian Orthodox Church. Their church officials rejected a number of the early edicts about the nature of Christ and Mary and do not recognize the authority of the Eastern Orthodox Patriarch. They have their own church leadership and those in Jordan are under the authority of their leaders in Jerusalem. Armenians in Jordan remain small in number but have come to dominate certain niches in the economy.

Historical Overview

Jordan like many countries of the Middle East is both old and new. The Hashemite Kingdom of Jordan officially dates from 1946 when it became independent, yet some of the oldest settlements in human history dating back to 8000 B.C. are also found in Jordan. Jordan is part of the ancient Fertile Crescent, which stretched from the southern borders of Palestine north to the Euphrates River and then down the course of the Euphrates and Tigris Rivers to the Persian Gulf. The region saw the rise of the Greek city-states called the Decapolis or the Ten Cities, which served to protect the eastern frontier during the Roman period. Jordan was the site of much of the New Testament and was the first part of the Byzantine Empire to become Muslim. The Crusaders built massive castles in Jordan only to lose them to Salah al-Din (Saladin) in the course of his re-conquest of Palestine. Jordan became a sleepy backwater of interest only to the tribal peoples living there until late in the Ottoman period when once again it became a place of activity with the expansion of civil rule, the settlement of non-Arab Circassians and Shishans, and the opening of the Hijaz Railway. In World War I, Arab-Bedouin troops commanded by their *shaykh*s and the British officer T. E. Lawrence (Lawrence of Arabia) made international news and captured Damascus ending centuries of Ottoman rule in the Arab world. Jordan became one of the important new states confronting Jewish immigration to Palestine and one of the major confrontation states with Israel after 1948. Modern Jordanian history has been dominated by the issue of Palestine and over one third of the country's population is Palestinian refugees.

FROM PREHISTORY TO THE ISLAMIC CONQUEST

Jordan is part of the Fertile Crescent where man first began to live in permanent settlements and made the change from hunter/gatherer to farmer and herdsman. Neolithic (8300 to 4500 B.C.) settlements dot Jordan's countryside and include some of the most important such as Tabqat Fahl (in the Jordan Valley), Baydah (north of Petra), 'Ayn Ghazal (a northern suburb of 'Amman), and Jericho (in the Jordan Valley). These settlements are referred to as "mega-sites" due to the fact that in sheer size they encompass ten to fifteen hectares, nearly twice as large as other Neolithic settlements.

Ancient Jordan was home to four Iron Age states, Edom, Moab, Rabboth Ammon, and Bashan. Bashan disappeared with the arrival of the Hebrew tribes under the command of Moses and Joshua who established themselves on both sides of the Jordan River sometime in the early Iron Age (around 1200 B.C.). Once the Hebrew tribes were organized into a state under King Saul (around 1025 B.C.), much of the ancient history of the region is marked by the conflicts between Israel and the Jordanian states of Rabboth Ammon, Moab, and Edom. Saul's successor David (1004 to 965 B.C.) brought them under his control, but later kings of Israel and Judah were unable to maintain their domination, especially over Moab and Edom.

While local history played out between the small kingdoms in Palestine and Jordan, the major powers of the day, Egypt and its eastern rivals the Hittites, the Assyrians, and later the Babylonians, saw the region as part of their spheres of influence. Egypt was usually able to keep Palestine and Jordan under its general domination as is testified to by numerous inscriptions and letters found in Egypt and Jordan. Egypt lost its domination first to the Assyrians who conquered Syria, Lebanon, Palestine, and Jordan in the period between 853 and 720 B.C. The Assyrians were unable to bring the unruly Bedouin tribes in the Syrian Desert fully under their rule, but were able to establish themselves in the major oases along the northern fringe of the desert. The Assyrians lost their empire to the Babylonians in 612 B.C. who also became major rivals of the Egyptians for control of Palestine and Jordan. The Babylonians conquered much of the region and in 588 B.C. destroyed the Kingdom of Judah taking many of the local people back to Babylon as slaves.

Both Egyptian and Babylonian power was broken by that of Persia in 539 B.C. when Cyrus the Great took Babylon and then in 530 B.C. his son Cambyses conquered Egypt unifying all of the eastern Mediterranean with the Persian heartlands in Iran. The Persians allowed the rebuilding of Jerusalem and the Jewish temple, but the Jewish dynasty that was installed remained weak and subordinate to the Satrap (or governor) appointed by the

Persian King. In Jordan, Bedouin tribes from the Arabian Peninsula such as the Nabateans were able to penetrate into settled areas and establish themselves at the expense of the older populations such as the Edomites whom they pushed out of their lands into southern Palestine.

The Persian Empire was conquered in 333 B.C. by Alexander the Great who briefly was able to unify the entire eastern Mediterranean from Greece to Egypt and east to the Indus River. Alexander died in Babylon in 323 B.C. and the empire was broken up and divided among his generals. The generals began to feud amongst themselves, and eventually Syria under the Seleucids, and Egypt under the Ptolemys, became the most important with Palestine and Jordan once again squeezed between larger rivals.

While the Nabateans became fully established in southern Jordan, the northern part of the country was settled by some 50,000 Greek soldiers distributed in ten cities called the Decapolis. This was done in 301 B.C. by Seleucus I Nicator with the expressed purpose of Hellenizing the region. Some of the cities in the Decapolis were ancient with their own local populations such as Rabboth Amon renamed Philadelphia while others were newly founded by the Greek soldiers such as Abila and Jarash.

While Syria and Egypt fought for domination over the region, local states arose often siding with one or other of the big powers. On the Palestinian side of the Jordan River, the Hasmoneans threw off Syrian control in 142 B.C. and remained free with the blessings of Ptolemaic Egypt. The Nabateans on the Jordanian side were in a better situation to remain beyond of the control of both powers. King Harith or Aretas III (86–62 B.C.) expanded Nabatean power and was able to even conquer the city of Damascus taking advantage of the on-going disputes of the greater regional powers.

In 64 B.C. Rome became involved in settling the dispute between Syria and Egypt forcing them to agree to a peace. While local dynasties were able to keep their thrones (at least for awhile), they did so as states bound to Rome with a Roman governor overseeing them. The Nabateans were still able to maintain their independence, and the rule of King Harith or Aretas IV (9 B.C. to 40 A.D.) marks the high point of Nabatean power and wealth. The Nabateans had taken control of the trade between Yemen and the Mediterranean supplying both the camels and their handlers. Nabatean merchants established commercial relationships in a wide network and as much as one-quarter of Rome's luxury trade in silks, spices, and incense passed through Nabatean hands.

The wealth of the Nabateans was their undoing. Rome could not let a small, independent kingdom exit both so close to its own borders and in control of so much of the luxury goods bound for the empire. The Nabateans were weakened as trade routes were encouraged to shift from the Red Sea and eastern Arabia to the Persian Gulf and the across the Syrian Desert to Damascus from Iraq. The cities of Hatra in Iraq and Tadmur or Palmyra in Syria eventually took much of the trade from Nabatean hands. In 106 A.D. the Roman Emperor Trajan annexed the Nabatean kingdom as the province Arabia Petrea placing it firmly under Roman control.

In the second and third centuries A.D. Rome established a line of fortifications to guard its eastern frontiers against the raids by Arab Bedouin and, more importantly, from the Persians after the rise of the vigorous Sassanian dynasty in 234. Initially such fortifications were manned by regular Roman soldiers but, as the empire began to decline local levies were raised to man them. By the sixth century those in Jordan were manned by Arab troops commanded by the local Ghassanid kings.

Christianity became the religion of the Roman Empire when in 313 the Emperor Constantine gave it official recognition. The Bani Ghassan became Christians and held the region on behalf of the Roman Emperors in Byzantium. Vassal Arab states such as the Bani Ghassan, allied to Byzantium, and the Lakhamids, allied to Persia, served as important buffers between the Byzantines and the Sassanids. Both kingdoms formed alliances with other Arab tribes bringing much of Arabia into the contest between the Byzantines and the Sassanids. Initially the advantage was with the Bani Ghassanids who defeated the Lakhamids in a number of small wars, but in 611 the Sassanids and their Arab allies launched an invasion of Syria, Lebanon, Palestine, and Jordan, which they occupied until 629 when the Byzantines and their Arab allies were able to finally push them back. As a reward for their help, the Byzantine Emperor Heraclius awarded the Bani Ghassan chief, Mundhir ibn Harith, the title "King of the Arabs." In the same year the Prophet Muhammad established treaties with the Christian and Jewish leaders of al-Aqabah, Maqnah, Udhrah, and al-Jarbah in southern Jordan. A new era in Jordanian and Arab history was beginning.

RISE OF ISLAM TO THE OTTOMANS

Islam came to Jordan during the lifetime of the Prophet Muhammad. The Prophet himself led the expedition to the northern Hijaz and southern Jordan between the years 629 and 630. He accepted the submission of the Jewish and Christian communities in southern Jordan while his military commander, Khalid ibn al-Walid, captured Jauf Oasis from the Ghassanids. Another column penetrated as far as the present day town of Mu'tah where a Byzantine force met them. The small Muslim force was defeated, but the conflict provided the faith with important martyrs including Ja'afar ibn Abi Talib, the younger brother of 'Ali and a cousin to the Prophet.

In 634 the Muslim armies returned to Jordan and crossed into Palestine where they defeated the Byzantines at Ajnadayn. In 636 the Byzantines made a concerted effort to retain their Syrian provinces, but at the Battle of Yarmuk the Muslims under Khalid ibn al-Walid inflicted a severe defeat and pushed the Byzantines north to Anatolia. The newly conquered territory was divided into four major provinces or *junds*, and Jordan was divided between the Jund of Filastin (Palestine) and the Jund of al-Urdunn (Jordan).

Jordan became embroiled in the disputes over leadership of the Muslim state supporting Mu'awiyah ibn Abi Sufyan against 'Ali ibn Abi Talib. The dispute ended with the assassination of 'Ali in 660 leaving Mu'awiyah the ruler of the emerging Islamic empire. Mu'awiyah and his descendants, the Umayyads, had their base of support in Syria (including much of Jordan) among the Bani Kalb Bedouin tribes. Keeping in close contact with them, the Umayyad princes spent much of their youth with the Bedouin perfecting their Arabic language skills and keeping free of the plagues found in cities such as the capital Damascus. Jordan's deserts have a large number of Umayyad pleasure palaces and hunting lodges where the princes were able to host Bedouin leaders or enjoy themselves after hunting.

The focus of the empire shifted to Iraq with the 'Abbasids who came to power in a bloody revolution in 750. The founder of the 'Abbasid dynasty, al-Saffah, ordered the death of all members of the Umayyad family and only a few were able to escape to the further reaches of the west eventually finding refuge in Muslim Spain. The power base of the 'Abbasids was in the east, Iraq and Iran, and they moved the capital from Damascus to the newly founded Baghdad where they could feel more secure.

Syria (including Jordan) was no longer a favored province but was instead seen as a possible place of revolt and unrest. There were a number of revolts against 'Abbasid rule and each time a revolt was crushed greater anti-'Abbasid sentiment grew among the Syrians. Anti-'Abbasid feelings were channeled into religion and Shi'ism was often the tool of this expression. In the 900s the radical Shi'ite Qaramitah movement became popular with many of the Bedouin and rural people in Syria, Jordan, and the Arabian Peninsula. The latter part of the 900s saw a number of Qaramitah attacks on urban centers in Syria and in 964 they were able to gain control of Palestine from the 'Abbasid governors of Egypt.

The 'Abbasids were further weakened when in 969 another Shi'ite movement from North Africa, the Fatimids, took Egypt and established their capital Cairo in 970. Jordan was once again caught between more powerful rivals in Egypt and Iraq. The Fatimids expanded into Palestine, Jordan, and southern Syria, and though the Saljuq Turks were eventually able to secure most of the region again in the name of the 'Abbasids. Palestine and Jordan remained the frontier with cities such as Jerusalem passing back and forth between the Fatimids and the Saljuqs several times. Jordan was of interest to these rival powers who wanted to control the major trade and pilgrimage routes from Damascus to Madinah and Makkah. The Fatimids were able to regain control of most of Palestine just before the First Crusade.

In 1095 Pope Urban II preached a holy Crusade to win the sites of early Christianity from the Saljuqs. The First Crusade eventually reached Jerusalem in 1099. The fall of Palestine and the whole Mediterranean coast of Syria and Lebanon to the Europeans made Jordan important to the Muslims, and as a result, to the Crusaders as well. In the first decades of the Latin Kingdom of Jerusalem, the Europeans pushed across the Jordan River and began to establish permanent fortifications to raid the trade between Damascus, the Hijaz, and Egypt. In 1115 a castle at Showbak called Montreal was built. Other, smaller castles were also built in southern Jordan and on the Island Graye or Jazirat al-Far'un in the Gulf of 'Aqabah to monitor and raid Muslim trade.

The Muslim response to the Latin states was slow in coming. The Crusaders suffered their first major defeat at the hands of the Saljuqs in 1119 near the northern Syrian city of Aleppo, but the Muslims did not follow up on their victory. The Saljuqs were fragmented into small, often bitter rival states with government in the hands of *Atabek*s, a combination of stepfather figure and prime minister. In the meantime the Latin Kingdom of Jerusalem expanded in Jordan ordering the construction of the massive fortress Pierre du Désert at Karak in 1142. The new fort became the seat of the Barony of Oultre-Jourdain, who controlled much of central and southern Jordan. Local Muslim and Christian communities were made subject to the Baron appointed by the King of Jerusalem.

The Kingdom of Jerusalem became an important regional power and entered into the political intrigues of the Fatimid court. King Amalric I supported the *Wazir* (or prime minister) Dirgham while Nur al-Din al-Zangi, the new ruler of a unified Syria, supported the deposed *Wazir* Shawar. After a long period of threats, counter threats, and invasions of Egypt, Nur al-Din and his lieutenant Salah al-Din al-Ayyubi (Saladin) were able to secure Egypt, thereby surrounding the Kingdom of Jerusalem. The routes in Jordan become more important to both the Muslims and the Crusaders as they were the main lines of communication between Damascus and Cairo. In order to strengthen Muslim control over the northern parts of Jordan that had not fallen under Crusader control, the fort at 'Ajlun was built in 1183 on the orders of Salah al-Din, who had succeeded Nur al-Din as sole ruler of Syria and Egypt in 1176.

Jordan became the scene for confrontation between the Latin Kingdom and Salah al-Din. Unfortunately for the Crusaders their King, Baldwin IV, was a leper, and his death left the crown to his sisters and their weak husbands. In addition, the Baron of Oultre-Jordain, Renaud de Châtillon, raided Muslim caravans including pilgrims on their way to Makkah. A raid on a caravan of Muslim pilgrims in 1187 broke the fragile truce with Salah al-Din. Listening to poor advice, King Guy of Jerusalem marched to meet the Muslims, and at the Horns of Hattin the Crusader army was defeated and nearly destroyed. With most of the military force gone, the city of Jerusalem surrendered soon afterwards. Salah al-Din proceeded to each of the Crusader forts and forced Karak to surrender in 1188 and Showbak in 1189 ending the Latin period in Jordanian history. Even though the Latin Kingdom was able to hang on for several more generations based in the Palestinian coastal city of Acre, the Crusaders never returned to Jordan.

When Salah al-Din died in 1193, his kingdom of unified Syria and Egypt was broken up among his brothers and sons. Power shifted from Damascus to Cairo while Jordan and most of Palestine were more frequently part of Egypt than of Syria. Major trade routes still passed through Jordan connecting the Red Sea and the Hijaz with Syria, Palestine, and Lebanon in the east and north with Egypt in west. Former Crusader fortifications were reused to guard the caravans, especially Showbak and Karak.

Jordan and Palestine were to become important again at the end of the Ayyubid dynasty. In 1249 al-Malik al-Salih Najm al-Din Ayyubi died leaving his wife Shajarat al-Durr (Spray of Pearls) as ruler. Shajarat al-Durr was forced to marry again and took as her husband one of Najm al-Din's Mamluks. Shajarat al-Durr was eventually murdered and her death marks the end of the Ayyubid dynasty and the beginning of the long period of Mamluk rule in Syria and Egypt (Bahri or Mongol/Turkish rulers from 1250 to 1382 and Burji or Circassian rulers from 1382 to 1517).

The Mamluks were slave soldiers who were purchased as boys and educated in military arts and sciences. Initially many of the boys came from Central Asia and were of Mongol or Turkish origins. Upon reaching manhood they would be freed yet would remain fiercely loyal to their former owners and commanders. They had come to replace local levies in a standing army around the Ayyubid princes and had proven themselves in battle against European Crusaders, decisively defeating the army of King Louis IX of France in 1250. They again proved their military prowess against the Mongol invasion of the Middle East and soundly defeated them in Palestine at the Battle of 'Ayn Jalut in 1260.

The first few years of Mamluk rule saw a quick succession of *amir*s until the rise of the Amir Baybars al-Bunduqdari. Baybars ruled Syria and Egypt from 1260 to 1277 from three capitals; Cairo, Damascus, and Karak. He had a number of former Crusader forts rebuilt and improved in order to protect trade and his lines of communication between Damascus and Cairo. Baybars ruled from horseback, frequently moving from one capital to another and spending a fair amount of time in Karak as the middle point between Syria and Egypt. When Baybars died, his immediate successor maintained all three capitals, but soon as Cairo emerged as the administrative capital, Karak and Damascus would both become provincial cities.

As long as a European Crusader state, no matter how small and weak, remained, the lines of communication and trade between Syria, the Hijaz, and Egypt would need to be protected. The final Crusader city of Acre fell in 1290 to the Mamluk Sultan al-Ashraf Khalil, and in 1301 the Sultan al-Nasir Muhammad defeated the Mongols ending the two major threats to security. Sultan al-Nasir Muhammad had sought retirement in Jordan and during his reign rebuilt Showbak and al-'Aqabah and built the shrine to Harun (Aaron, elder brother of Moses) in the mountains south of Petra.

The Black Death and misrule by Bahri sultans helped cause their downfall. A six-year-old child was placed on the throne by scheming *amir*s amid palace revolutions, and eventually the Amir Barquq took the throne and became the first of the Burji Sultans. Through the long period of Burji control, Jordan was part of Egypt, administered by Cairo. But for the most part, Jordan lost its importance except for the yearly pilgrimage to Makkah. The Mamluks were in slow decline until al-Ashraf Qansu al-Ghawri took the throne in 1501. Al-Ghawri was a vigorous ruler but in 1502 the Bedouin tribes in Jordan rose in revolt. By 1505 the Bedouin had pushed across into Palestine and attacked Jerusalem. Al-Ghawri was eventually able to raise the Syrian *amir*s to action and put down the rebellion, however, a new far more dangerous threat was rising in the north.

In 1516 the Ottoman Sultan Salim Yavuz or the Grim turned his attentions south to the Mamluks. At Marj Dabiq outside of Aleppo he inflicted a crippling blow to the Mamluks and the Sultan al-Ghawri died in the fighting. In 1517 the Ottomans defeated the Mamluks outside of Cairo and Egypt, Jordan, and the Hijaz became part of the expanding Ottoman Empire.

Like the Mamluks before them, the Ottoman's main interest in Jordan was the annual pilgrimage to Makkah and little else. A rebellion in Karak during the reign of Sulayman the Magnificent (1520–66) was successful in establishing the al-Nimr family from Nablus as local lords and they remained outside of direct Ottoman control. A rebellion of Bedouin tribes around Showbak at the same time ended Turkish rule there for a time.

The Ottomans were primarily interested in the pilgrim routes from Damascus and Cairo and Sultan Sulayman had a new route built. Forts were built at Ma'an, al-Qatrani, al-Hasa, and 'Anayzah manned by small Turkish units. Sulayman also began the Ottoman policy of paying Bedouin *shaykhs* cash subsidies in order to ensure the safe passage of the pilgrim caravans.

Most of Jordan was ignored, forcing local farming communities to fend for themselves against the Bedouin. Local families and lineages grouped themselves together in tribe-like organizations encompassing a number of villages that became known as the *nahiyah*s or districts. Twelve districts emerged each administered by a council of elders under the general authority of a district leader or *shaykh*. The villages were organized to be able to respond to a Bedouin raid by providing men and weapons under the leadership of the district *qa'id* or military commander. The villagers began to take on many of the cultural values of the Bedouin, even to adopt aspects of their Arabic dialect, setting them off from their settled cousins a short distance away to the west in Palestine.

Ottoman attention was drawn to Jordan with the occupation of Syria by Muhammad 'Ali, governor of Egypt, from 1830 to 1841. During their brief period of rule, the Egyptians tried to establish order and control the Bedouin tribes. In 1834 a revolt began in Jordan centered first in Karak. The Egyptians were able to retake Karak, but the revolt continued in other parts of the country. Eventually the revolt was crushed but the Egyptians were forced to leave Syria in 1841 due to pressure from the major European powers.

RETURN OF OTTOMAN AUTHORITY TO WORLD WAR I

The Ottomans returned to Jordan first at the request of the people of the Wastiyah Nahiyah, who had asked for help against the Bedouin al-Sa'adi tribe in 1840/41. The Turkish governor of Damascus sent troops to conquer the Bedouin, and it is said that the Bedouin were destroyed to nearly the last man. In 1851 the Turks established a *sanjaq* or administrative district in Irbid under the *mutasarrifiyyah* (a larger administrative region) of Nablus in Palestine, which in turn was responsible to the governor in Damascus. The Sanjaq of Irbid included most of the 'Ajlun region south to the Zarqa' River. The Ottomans further strengthened their control over the region by settling Circassian and Shishan refuges from the Caucasus, as well as Turkomen in places such as Jarash, Suwaylah, Wadi al-Sir, Umm Ruman, and Na'ur. The Circassians and Shishans were able to defend themselves and their villages from raids by Bedouin and forced the Bedouin further back into the desert.

Ottoman authority was eventually invited back to Karak in 1893 by the *shaykh* of the powerful Majali family. The Turks expanded south and organized the region into another *sanjaq* called the Sanjaq of Karak under the governor of Damascus. Only the Port of al-'Aqabah was not included as it fell under the control of the governor of Madinah. In 1900, work began on the Hijaz Railway linking Damascus eventually with Madinah in Arabia. Bedouin tribes, who had come to rely on yearly subsidies paid to them by the pilgrim caravans or who had gained the right to supply these caravans with camels and guides, were opposed to the railway. Other tribes in Jordan were also hostile to the railway because it meant Turkish troops could be deployed quickly to any place along the route. Work on the construction of the railway was slow due to raids by the Bedouin, but by 1906 it had reached 'Amman, and two years later it was completed all the way to Madinah. Southern Jordan experienced the last local revolts against the Turks, in 1905 in Showbak and 1910 in Karak. Both were crushed and the leaders of the 1910 revolt were hanged in public, an action that greatly angered the local people and became an important cause for their support of the Arab Revolt a few years later. Peace did not last long. In 1914 World War I began and the Turks sided with Germany and Austria.

Discontent with the Turkish government had been growing in the Arab provinces of the empire starting in the mid-1800s. Young Arabs sought higher education in Europe or went to Christian-mission schools (many of which were American) that had been established in Lebanon and Palestine. In Europe, Arabs from Syria, Palestine, Lebanon, and Egypt met and formed social and political clubs to discuss the affairs in the Turkish Empire. Once back in the empire they continued their activities, and in 1909 the most influential of these clubs, al-Muntada al-Adabi, was founded in Istanbul by Arabs working in the Turkish government. The future *Sharif* of Makkah, Hussein ibn 'Ali, was among the Arab activists, and even while under "invitation" by the Sultan to live in Istanbul, kept up his contacts with other Arab political activists. While educated Arabs were organizing themselves, a similar movement was happening among the educated Turkish elites called the Committee for Union and Progress (CUP)or the Young Turks. In 1908 the CUP instigated a military revolt and forced the Sultan 'Abd al-Hamid II to grant a constitution, abolish censorship, and release political prisoners. A year later the Sultan tried to regain power, but was defeated and deposed, and a distant cousin, Muhammad V Rashad was made the new Sultan. Among the first acts of the new government was to appoint Hussein ibn 'Ali as Sharif of Makkah and he and his three sons, Faysal, 'Ali, and 'Abdallah left Istanbul for Arabia.

In 1912 'Abdallah was elected to the new parliament and on the way to Istanbul stopped in Cairo to confer with the British High Commissioner Sir Herbert Kitchener. 'Abdallah was to sound out British opinion should the Arabs rise in revolt against the Turks. The Turkish government was aware of 'Abdallah's nationalist activities and his visit to Cairo and tried to buy his friendship by giving him the governorship of Yemen. However, in 1914, just prior to the outbreak of World War I, he was again in contact with Kitchener in Cairo.

The British wanted to maintain an open dialogue with the Arab nationalists especially after the close relationship grew between Germany and Turks. Kaiser Wilhelm II had visited Palestine in 1898, and Germany had offered to build the Berlin to Baghdad Railway, which the British opposed. The close relationship between the Germans and Turks continued after the fall of Sultan 'Abd al-Hamid II, and in 1914 the Turks sided with Germany in the war. When the war broke out, the Arab citizens of the empire were not strongly sympathetic to the Turks, although most assisted the Turkish state as was required of them. The British had maintained their own connections with the Arabs through a series of letters between Sir Henry MacMahon, British High Commissioner for Egypt, and Sharif Hussein in Makkah and, though vaguely worded, the Sharif thought that he had British assurances of an Arab state that would embrace all of the Arab provinces of the Ottoman Empire. In June 1916 Sharif Hussein launched the Arab Revolt unaware that the British had earlier struck a deal with France, the Sykes-Picot Agreement, to divide the Turkish Empire between them after the war.

The Arab Revolt had initial success in Makkah and Ta'if, but the Turkish garrison in Madinah was able to resist the attack. The British sent military advisors including the legendary T. E. Lawrence, Lawrence of Arabia, to help the Arabs. Turkish garrisons in Arabia were left besieged by armies under 'Ali and 'Abdallah while Faysal and Lawrence took an army north to Jordan where the local tribal *shaykh*s joined them. With the help of Huwaytat tribe under their Shaykh 'Awdah Abu Tayy, the Turkish fort at al-'Aqabah was taken in 1917. The Arab army pushed on to take Showbak and Tafilah the same year. In the meantime, the British had pushed forward taking southern Palestine as far north as Jerusalem. The Arab army under Lawrence liberated Damascus, and by October 1918 the Arabs and British forces had pushed the Turks as far north as Anatolia before an armistice was signed.

FOUNDING OF THE AMIRATE TO THE PRESENT DAY

Following the victory of the Arab and British armies, the Arabs began to organize a government in Damascus with Faysal as King of Syria. The French, however, pressed for their share of the empire, which included Syria, and at the Peace Conference in Versailles Arab hopes were sacrificed to European interests. Britain and France were awarded most of the Arab provinces as Mandates, with France taking Syria and Lebanon and Britain taking Palestine (which included the Transjordan) and Iraq. The Arabs were left with little other than Hijaz ruled by men loyal to Faysal. Faysal had been declared the King of Syria by the Syrian Parliament and troops were raised to defend their new state. In addition, Faysal's brother 'Abdallah was raising troops in Arabia to assist in the defense. The French invaded in 1920 and at Maysalun outside of Damascus defeated the Syrians. Faysal was forced to leave Damascus, but meanwhile his brother 'Abdallah arrived in southern Jordan in November of that year with an army to restore Faysal to the Syrian throne. 'Abdallah moved north through Karak to 'Amman, where he was invited by Winston Churchill to meet with the new British High Commissioner for Palestine, Sir Herbert Samuel. Samuel had tried to set up a number of small, local governments in Transjordan but they had all collapsed in chaos. He proposed to separate the Transjordan from Palestine (the region was seen as too tribal to be ruled together with the mainly non-tribal people of Palestine) and give it to 'Abdallah to administer, in lieu of 'Abdallah's support for his brother's claim to Syria. The British also proposed to Faysal that he take the throne of Iraq and give up his claims to Syria. Both brothers agreed; 'Abdallah gaining the Amirate of the Transjordan and Faysal, the Hashemite Kingdom of Iraq.

At first 'Abdallah was still very hostile to the French in Syria, and his new capital, 'Amman, attracted a large number of Syrian nationalists. 'Abdallah allowed them to conduct raids across the border; however, the British could not allow this to continue and put pressure on 'Abdallah and forced him to end the raids. 'Abdallah faced more serious threats to his rule from within Jordan, where both settled villagers and Bedouin tribes refused to pay taxes or recognize his government. 'Abdallah had to deal with a number of local revolts, but quickly gained the respect and support of the tribes through his quick show of force and of forgiveness. He allowed a British officer, Frederick Peake, to raise an army from mainly the settled *hadar* population called the Arab Army (later called the Arab Legion), which he used to put down revolts. The Arab Army was well-trained and could respond quickly to any threat.

While 'Abdallah was able to quickly deal with the internal threats to his rule, he was faced with a far more dangerous foe across the border in Saudi Arabia. 'Abd al-'Aziz ibn Sa'ud had been able to restore his family to power by taking their former capital Riyadh from the Shammar al-Rashid governor in 1902. Once he had been able to retake the Sa'udi heartland he embarked on a policy of both political and religious expansion conquering the Qasim in 1906, Hassa in 1913, and the Hijaz in 1925. At first the British paid little attention, but the successes of the ibn Sa'ud's *Ikhwan* (or Brotherhood) forces came to the attention of the India Office and Britain recognized ibn Sa'ud's government in 1915. The India Office supported ibn Sa'ud while the Foreign Office supported the Hashemites in the Hijaz, Iraq, and Jordan. Sa'udi *Ikhwan* raids into Jordan took on the appearance of major expeditions and in 1924 they came to within five miles (seven kilometers) of 'Amman before being detected and driven back.

Tensions continued between the two countries as Bedouin from both sides of the border launched raids and counter raids against each other. The Jordanian tribes suffered the most. In 1925 the Sirhan tribe lost most of their camels and in 1930 a section of the Huwaytat lost their tents, flocks, and herds to Sa'udi Bedouin forces. In order to protect Jordan's borders, a new unit was organized called the Transjordanian Frontier Force seconded from the Palestinian Police Force. Even though the force was mechanized, it proved unable to deal with the Bedouin raiders. The British officer John Bagot Glubb stationed in Iraq was contacted to recruit a military force from the Jordanian Bedouin similar to the Bedouin force he had organized in Iraq. Called the Desert Patrol Force, the new unit was able to finally bring an end to the raids from Saudi Arabia as well as keep the peace between Jordanian tribes. King ibn Sa'ud had become aware the potential threat the *Ikhwan* posed to his own government and brought a final end to them in 1930.

Jewish immigration in Palestine began before World War I, but the numbers greatly increased following the war. Tensions between the European Jews and the Palestinian Arabs grew with clashes in several Palestinian cities. In 1936 the Palestinians rose in revolt and many Jordanians sympathized with them. Palestinian agents were sent to the 'Ajlun to recruit soldiers but were they rounded up and sent back by the Arab Legion. 'Abdallah supported the British White Paper of 1939, which called for a mixed Arab and Jewish population in Palestine and limited Jewish immigration, but proposed that Palestine be placed under him to govern. 'Abdallah had never given up the idea of a unified Syria and kept close contact with supporters in Syria and Palestine. However, during the Mandate period, the republicans gained the initiative over 'Abdallah's supporters in both Syria and Palestine forcing him to give up his dream of a unified (Hashemite) Syria.

World War II caused a respite in the Palestine problem and Jordan's armed forces participated in several operations in Syria and Iraq alongside British troops. Once the war ended Jordan, along with Lebanon and Syria, became fully independent and Jordan renamed itself the Hashemite Kingdom of Jordan in 1946. No sooner was Jordan independent than the issue of Palestine was reopened as large numbers of European Jews attempted to immigrate. Attempts to find a settlement to the dispute by the newly formed United Nations came to nothing and eventually Britain as the Mandate power withdrew and Israel declared itself an independent state in 1948. In response the Arab states of Egypt, Lebanon, Syria, and Jordan invaded to uphold the rights of the Palestinians. The Arabs were not adequately prepared for war; their armies were poorly equipped and most of their troops were poorly trained. Only the Jordanians had success and held the West Bank and the old city of Jerusalem against determined attacks. The Egyptians were able to maintain only the Gaza Strip, and the Syrians and Lebanese were pushed out of Palestine. The fighting came to an end in 1949 and a cease fire was signed between all parties establishing de facto borders. Thousands of Palestinians from the areas controlled by Israel became refugees, filling camps set up for them by the United Nations in the Gaza Strip, the West Bank, Lebanon, Syria, and Jordan.

The failure of the Palestinian leadership before and during the conflict with Israel lost them the respect of not only their own people, but of the other Arab leaders. The Palestinian people were in a serious position; they had no one to be their recognized spokesman. King 'Abdallah hoping to revive the old dream of a unified Hashemite Syria had the Jordanian parliament pass the Act of Unification in 1950 making the West Bank part of the Kingdom. Palestinians from the West Bank became Jordanians with full citizenship and passports whether they wanted it or not. For many Palestinians this was not welcomed; they wanted to be Palestinians with their own country, not be to made citizens of another country. In addition, for many Palestinians, Jordanians were rude, backwoods country folk lacking in sophistication and education. The cultural gap between the two peoples had grown even wider during the Mandate period. Politically, most Palestinians did not want a monarchy, but had hoped for a representational republican system of their own. In 1951 while in Jerusalem, King 'Abdallah was assassinated by a young Palestinian nationalist.

King 'Abdallah was succeeded by his son Talal, however Talal suffered from a mental condition, and there was strong pressure from the British and from within the Hashemite family for him to abdicate in favor of his young son Hussein. Talal abdicated in 1952 and in 1953 Hussein became King. The young king was faced with a number of problems in the wake of the 1948 war with Israel. The poor showing of especially the Egyptian army had been due to inept high ranking officers and serious corruption in the government. Attempts by King Faruq's government to deal with these problems were made, but they were too little too late. In 1952 Faruq was deposed in a military coup by a group of young officers, including Gamal 'Abd al-Nasir and Anwar al-Saddat. The Arab world was humiliated by the defeat in Palestine, and a new wave of Arab nationalism swept the region embodied in men like 'Abd al-Nasir.

Jordan still had British military bases on its soil and the Jordanian army was commanded by a British officer, John Bagot Glubb or Glubb Pasha. Despite the fact that the Jordanians had done better than the other Arab armies in the 1948 war, the presence of British military on Arab soil was a focal point of anger for Arab nationalists. This was all the more so when the British, French, and Israelis attacked Egypt in 1956 after 'Abd al-Nasir nationalized the Suez Canal. King Hussein dismissed Glubb and the forced the British to close their bases in Jordan. This was not enough for the pro-Nasir nationalists in Jordan and between 1956 and 1958 there was a struggle between them and King Hussein for control of Jordan. Elections in 1956 swept in a national-ist parliament with Sulayman Nablusi, head of the National Socialist Party, asked to form a new government. In a subsequent test of power the King won using the strong support he had from the Bedouin dominated army. The par-liament was dismissed in 1957 and a subsequent coup attempt was crushed by the Bedouin troops.

In 1958 Egypt and Syria formed the United Arab Republic as a step towards the long-dreamed-for unity for the Arab people. In response the two Hashemite Kingdoms, Jordan and Iraq formed the Arab Federation, but it was quickly dissolved when the Hashemites in Iraq lost their throne in a bloody revolution in the same year. The United Arab Republic collapsed in 1961 when Syria withdrew over problems of Egyptian abuse of power inside Syria. King Hussein had lost the support of his cousins in Iraq and began forging other relationships opening up to the Saudis and others who were not comfortable with 'Abd al-Nasir's popularity with the Arab people.

During this time the Palestinian refugees in the camps and had to orga-nize themselves as best as they could. The old social and political order had crumbled in the 1948 war and a new leadership needed to emerge. Taking the initiative, the Egyptians pushed for the formation of the Palestine Libera-tion Organization (PLO)—separate from the Jordanians—at the first Arab Summit in 1964. A tool of the Egyptians, the first PLO had little popular support from the Palestinians themselves. Instead, organizations born in the refugee camps like al-Fath gained greater respect and support. These organi-zations launched raids across the Egyptian and Jordanian frontiers to attack targets inside Israel. While they were not able to do much damage, they did provoke the Israelis into severe cross-border retaliations. In 1966 the Israelis raided into the Jordanian-held West Bank and forced King Hussein into closer relations with both Syria and Egypt. In 1967 King Hussein, pledging mutual assistance if attacked by Israel, signed the Joint Defense Pact with Egypt and Syria.

In June of 1967 the confrontation between Egypt and Israel over use of the Suez Canal erupted into war and within six days the Egyptians, Syrians, and Jordanians were not only defeated but had lost large amounts of terri-tory. Once again Jordan received Palestinian refugees, some made refugee for a second time. While the Jordanian army was defeated and forced to retreat to the East Bank of the Jordan River, it had been able to do so in good order and with minimal loss. The Israelis flushed with their quick victory over three Arab armies, felt they could operate as they pleased and in 1968 crossed the Jordan River to destroy the Palestinian guerillas at Karamah in the Jordan Valley. They were surprised to find the Palestinian fighters did not retreat but fought back inflicting losses on the Israelis. Alerted to the attack, the Jordanian army responded, using tanks and artillery to force the Israelis to withdraw. The defeat of the Israelis encouraged the Palestinian commandos who continued to launch raids across the river. In 1968 the al-Fath movement took over control of the PLO, breaking Egypt's control of the organization. The Palestinians were on the way to be their own voice in their conflict with Israel.

Jordan was one of the most important confrontation states with both a long border with Israel and a large portion of its population Palestinians. Palestinian camps began to operate with their own local government controlled by armed men from groups like al-Fath. Jordanian authority was ignored, increasing frictions between Jordanian police and military on one hand, and with the Palestinians on the other. The situation came to a head in September 1970 when the PFLP (Popular Front for the Liberation of Palastine), which is a different organization from the PLO, hijacked a number of international airlines and brought them to an abandoned airbase near Mafraq in the northern desert. The hijackers eventually released the hostages and blew up the planes, but the Jordanian army could take no more from the Palestinian fighters. The army and the fighters fought a brief but fierce battle to control 'Amman and in the end the army prevailed in what has come to be called Black September. The conflict was mediated in Cairo by 'Abd al-Nasir and King Hussein and Yasir 'Arafat agreed to end the fighting. The Palestinian fighters were forced to leave the country and many sought refuge in Lebanon. By 1971 the last of the fighters had been forced to leave.

Following Black September Jordan embarked on a policy to "Jordanianize" the civil service and the army. A glass ceiling was imposed on promotions for Palestinians and many of those who had risen to high ranks were fired or retired. East Bankers were promoted, sometimes over better qualified Palestinian candidates. Sensitive police and military command positions went to men of Bedouin or Circassian origins whose loyalty was not in question. Police and military checkpoints were set up to control and monitor the movements of Palestinians within Jordan, especially to points such as the port of al-'Aqabah and the Jordan Valley.

Jordan stayed out of the 1973 war with Israel but offered material support to the Syrians. Jordan lost an important diplomatic battle to the PLO headed by Yasir 'Arafat when in 1974 the Arab League recognized them as the sole legitimate voice of the Palestinian people. Jordan still remained one of the most important confrontation states with Israel and technically still had legitimate sovereignty over the occupied West Bank. In 1976 the Palestinian leader Yasir 'Arafat meet with King Hussein and began to rebuild relations destroyed in 1970 and, in the wake of the Camp David Accords between Egypt and Israel, the 1978 Baghdad Arab Summit pledged massive economic assistance for Jordan's steadfastness in the struggle with Israel.

Since the Act of Unification in 1950 Jordan had administered the West Bank paying the salaries of its civil servants, even after the 1967 war. When the Arab League recognized the PLO as the legitimate voice of the Palestinian people, the Jordanians began the disengagement process. The parliament representing both banks of Jordan was abrogated in 1974. While technically still part of Jordan, the West Bank was slowly being cut loose. By 1981 a new leadership was emerging on the West Bank of locally elected officers, but the Israeli Defense Force, fearing the growth of Palestinian self-government, crushed the movement.

The decade of the 1980s saw the final withdrawal of the Israelis from Egyptian Sinai, the Lebanese civil war plunge into further depths, and two Israeli invasions of Lebanon. Jordan was still a major party to the conflict, though it was also able to take advantage of the continued Lebanese civil war to emerge as the new financial capital replacing Beirut. Jordan was one of the few pro-Western Arab states and had an open market and a stable currency. In the period of 1981 to 1984 when Israel was introducing free trade and liberalization policies, the Jordanian dinar, along with the U.S. dollar, was briefly used instead of the Israeli shekel. 'Amman became an important commercial center for international trade in the Middle East. Jordan's people reached high levels of education, and illiteracy dropped to 15 percent, composed of mainly the elderly. Jordanians found work in the Arab Gulf states and Saudi Arabia and were preferred over the more politically active Palestinians. Jordanian Bedouin were hired by the governments of Kuwait and Bahrain to serve as police or in the military.

Israel's invasion of Lebanon in 1982 was supposed to be to bring peace to the northern border areas that had been the target of Palestinian attacks. Once in Lebanon, the Israeli command thought they would be able to crush the PLO and the Palestinians, and they pushed to Beirut, which was subjected to intense shelling. The Palestinian fighters once more were forced to leave, and this time refuge was granted to them in Tunisia. It seemed for awhile that the Palestinian dream was even further away from reality, but in 1984 the Palestinian National Council met in 'Amman. In 1985 the Jordanians and Palestinians agreed to coordinate peace negotiations. Much to everyone's surprise, the Palestinian Uprising (or *Intifadah*) began in 1987. No one seemed to be in charge yet it continued despite the best efforts by the Israeli Defense

Force to crush it. The young men and women who led the grassroots uprising did not depend on outside assistance nor did they take orders from the exiled Palestinian leadership. Jordan took a final step in its separation from the West Bank and in 1988 withdrew all of its administrative and legal ties. The West Bank became responsibility of the Palestinians.

Despite the fact that Jordan had replaced Beirut as the financial center for the Middle East, its economy based on agriculture and phosphates was stumbling. In 1989 Jordan embarked on the International Monetary Fund's program for structural readjustment. The Jordanian dinar fell against the U.S. dollar from slightly over three U.S. dollars to the dinar to slightly under one U.S. dollar to the dinar. Prices rose as the value of the dinar fell causing riots to erupt in the Bedouin-dominated southern town of Ma'an. In the same year Jordan allowed the first open, free, and fair elections since 1956, and the Islamists won a clear majority throughout the country.

Following the confrontation with the Nasirist nationalists in the 1950s, the Jordanian government found the Muslim Brotherhood and other Islamic parties to be political allies. The Muslim Brotherhood had no love for 'Abd al-Nasir after he began to arrest and persecute them in Egypt. King Hussein saw the possibilities of an alliance with the Islamists and encouraged them as a foil to not only the nationalists but also the leftists among mainly the Palestinians. As a result the Islamist parties did not need to worry about government interference and by the end of the 1980s were among the strongest political parties in the country. It was no surprise they won the first open and free elections in 1989.

Iraq's invasion of Kuwait in 1990 further complicated an already complicated state of affairs in the Middle East. Kuwait had little sympathy from the majority of Arabs. They and other oil-rich Gulf Arabs and Saudis had established poor reputations because of their bad behavior abroad and for the poor way they treated those Arabs working in their countries. King Hussein initially tried to mediate the problem and get Saddam Hussein to withdraw. However, Saddam Hussein refused to withdraw his forces, and in 1991 the United States and its allies (including Egypt and Syria) launched the counteroffensive and pushed the Iraqi forces out of Kuwait and into southern Iraq. King Hussein did not seem to take a strong stance against Iraq during the war, therefore the Gulf countries and Saudi Arabia decided to punish Jordan for this. Jordanians working in the Gulf and Saudi Arabia were fired and forced to return to Jordan. It was worse for Jordanians and Palestinians in Kuwait where they were seen to be collaborators with the Iraqis. The arrival of a large number of Jordanians (and Palestinians) added to the economic problems of the country. Nearly all of them were well educated but there were no jobs for them.

Jordan participated in the Madrid summit and embarked on the road to a peace treaty with Israel. This was signed in 1994, formally ending hostilities and opening up full diplomatic relations and an exchange of ambassadors between the two countries. The border was open to travel, tourism, and economic trade. While peace officially existed between Jordan and Israel, few Jordanians embraced it. Israeli tourists increased the need for strong security, and popular destinations such as Petra seemed to swarm with Jordanian security forces. Israeli tourism began to slow after a few shootings and stopped nearly altogether in 2000 when the second Palestinian *Intifadah* began.

The Oslo talks between the Israelis and Palestinians set the framework for the Madrid summit. The United States needed to demonstrate a real desire to settle the Palestinian-Israeli conflict after the Gulf War in 1991. The Palestinian leadership had supported Saddam Hussein in the war, and now had to make up with other parties involved. In 1992 Jordan, the Palestinians, and Israel held talks in Washington, DC and, as noted above, Jordan signed a peace treaty with Israel in 1994. Yasir 'Arafat returned to the Occupied Territories and set up the Palestinian Authority. A provocative visit to the Dome of the Rock and al-Aqsa Mosque by Israeli politician Ariel Sharon sparked the second Palestinian *Intifadah* and the eventual showdown between Yasir 'Arafat and the Israelis.

The troubled relationship between the Palestinians and the Israelis dominated the last years of King Hussein's life. Sick with cancer the King remained active as much as possible. In 1999 Hussein had the Jordanian constitution changed to allow his son 'Abdallah (from his second marriage to a British woman) to succeed the throne rather than the King's younger brother Hasan. A month later Hussein died after he became chilled during an open-car parade celebrating his return to Jordan after cancer treatment abroad. His son 'Abdallah succeeded to the throne as King 'Abdallah II and his younger brother Hamzah (from Hussein's third marriage to a Palestinian woman) became the Crown Prince.

'Abdallah II is one of a number of young Arab leaders coming to power in recent years. Many of the old guard in the government were retired and a new cadre of young technocrats were recruited. Jordan under 'Abdallah II remains a key country in the region. When the United States invaded Iraq in 2003 the majority of Jordanians opposed the war fueling strong anti-American feelings. Various claims made by the Bush administration to justify the invasion did not convince the Jordanian people, and while the Jordanian government did not take an active stand against the invasion, Jordanian television coverage was openly hostile.

Once the main fighting was over, the Jordanian government began efforts to repair whatever damage may have been done to their relationship with both the United States and Britain as result of the war. Jordan has been a staunch ally in the War Against Terror since the September 11th attack in New York City, even during the U.S.-led invasion of Iraq, and remains so. There is an active exchange of information between the two countries and when the American ships docked at al-'Aqabah were fired upon in September 2005 the Jordanians responded quickly with arrests within a day of the attack. In November of 2005 Jordan suffered its own version of September 11th with suicide bombings in three hotels. The suicide bombers targeted three hotels where foreigners were known to stay, yet 33 of the 56 people killed were Jordanians, and most of them were guests at two Jordanian wedding parties. The Jordanian authorities arrested a fourth bomber whose device had not gone off, and from her it was discovered all four were Iraqis recruited by Abu Musa'b al-Zarqawi, head of the al-Qa'idah network in Iraq. The suicide attacks left Jordanians stunned; however, starting the following night ordinary citizens rallied to support the government and to condemn the attacks.

CONCLUSION

The geography of Jordan influenced and still influences the culture and history of its people. With around 80 percent of the country desert and fit mainly for pastoral nomadism, the Bedouin have come to define much of what is "Jordanian". The narrow band of agricultural lands running along the eastern rim of the Rift Valley system has either been under the control of larger regional powers such as Egypt, Syria, or Iraq, or have been left to fend for themselves with their Bedouin neighbors.

Since World War I Jordan has been pulled into the conflict between the Palestinians and Jewish immigrants, and after World War II into the wider regional conflict that erupted with the establishment of Israel in 1948. Jordan has been the country where the largest numbers of Palestinians have gone as refugees putting strains on its fragile economy and politics. The ripple effect caused by the creation of Israel and the mass movement of large numbers of displaced Palestinians has been the root cause for much of the instability in the Middle East. The fall of the Shah of Iran in 1979 to a populist Islamic revolution destabilized much of the Gulf region leading to the destructive and protracted Iran-Iraq War and eventually to the 1990–91 and 2003 Gulf Wars, which resulted in the eventual fall of Iraqi President Saddam Hussein.

Despite the reoccurring instability in the region, Jordan, guided by King Hussein, was able to remain an island of stability through the volatile period of modern Middle Eastern history. Jordan has remained one of the few stable countries in the region, being able to weather political and economic storms. Much of Jordan's success was due to the abilities of King Hussein, and now it is his son 'Abdallah II's turn to demonstrate his ability to do the same.

2

Religion and World View

Over 80 percent of Jordanians are Sunni Muslims and most of the remainder are Christians, belonging to a number of different denominations. Since the Syrian Revolt of 1925, a small number of Druze live in some of the northern towns around Azraq. When Jordan administered the West Bank, it also numbered among its people the Samaritans, a Jewish sect that has survived since before the time of Christ. Jordan's different religious communities are found in most of the country, though the Christians are more frequently found in the larger towns and cities. However, Jordan is one of the few countries of the Middle East where there are Christian Bedouin. These Christian Bedouin live near Karak and claim to be the direct descendants of the Bani Ghassan tribe who ruled the region for the Byzantines prior to the arrival of Islam in 630.

ISLAM IN JORDAN

The overwhelming number of Jordanians are Sunni Muslims following the Shafi'i School or *Madhhab*. The division between Sunni and Shi'i began in the early centuries of the religion as a dispute over who should be considered the legitimate successor to the Prophet Muhammad and leader of the Muslim community, but has come today to include differences in sources of and application of Islamic law or the *Shari'ah*. Within Sunni Islam there are four Schools of Law, each named for the person who founded and began the work to codify it. The majority of Jordanians belong to the Shafi'i School named for the late eighth- to early ninth-century Islamic scholar Muhammad bin Idris al-Shafi'i (died 820). The Shafi'i School is the main one found in most of the Arabic-speaking Middle East from Egypt eastward and is shared with the majority of Sunnis in Syria, Lebanon, Iraq, and Egypt. In addition to the Shafi'i School, Shishan, Circassian, Uzbek, and Turkomen Jordanians belong to the Hanafi School, which is spread mainly among the Turkish-speaking areas of Anatolia and Central Asia as well as the Caucasus. Because it was the school of the ruling Ottoman Turkish elite, it is also found in the former provinces of the Ottoman Empire. The Hanafi School was founded earlier than the Shafi'i by the Islamic scholar Abu Hanifa (died 767).

The Shafi'i School differs from the other three in the importance given to the main sources of Islamic law. For al-Shafi'i there were four sources for legal decisions, the Qur'an, the *Sunnah* of the Prophet, which includes *Hadith* (or sayings attributed to him as well as his actions), analogy (or *qiyas*), and finally consensus (or *ijma'*). While most of the Islamic schools of law use the same sources, the order of use is not the same and for al-Shafi'i any contradiction or seeming contradiction between the Qur'an (the word of God) and the Sunnah (actions and words of the Prophet of God) were to be seen within their own contexts. That is, the Sunnah is to help understand the meaning of the Qur'an and if some action or word of the Prophet is found to be in contradiction to the revelations of the Qur'an, there would also be another action or statement of the Prophet that would support the Qur'an. Al-Shafi'i helped systematize the use of analogy, and he is thought by many to be the first to truly provide a system for Islamic jurisprudence.

The Hanafi School of Law began just prior to the Shafi'i and according to legend Abu Hanifa died the same day that al-Shafi'i was born. Abu Hanifa was a leading Islamic scholar in the Iraqi city Kufa and tended to reflect the attitudes of the emerging Islamic society, which combined legal concepts from Roman law with that of Arabia. The four major sources of Islamic law are the same as those discussed by al-Shafi'i, however, the source and its priority differ in the application to a particular legal case.

There is a small number of Druze in Jordan as a result of the 1925 Revolt in Syria against the French. Sultan al-Atrash, the leader of the Syrian Druze in Jabal Druze, rose in revolt against the French. His revolt was eventually crushed, but during the fighting a number of Druze families relocated to several northern Jordanian towns and villages not far from the Syrian border.

Druze are considered to be a heterodox group within Islam, that is, their religion is derived from the major principles of Islam, but has greatly deviated from them. For many Muslims, the Druze are outside of the faith and not considered to be Muslims. The Druze religion was founded during the lifetime of the Fatimid Khalifah al-Hakim bi-Amr Allah (996–1024) who was named the *Imam* (head of the Muslim community) and the *'Aqil* (or Cosmic Intellect). The religious movement took its name from one of al-Hakim's most faithful adherents and missionaries, al-Darazi. Al-Hakim was assassinated, some say by his own sister who could no longer tolerate his erratic behavior. Al-Hakim's followers were forced to seek refuge in the mountains of Lebanon where they were able to establish a community. For the Druze, al-Hakim did not die but went into a state of suspended animation from which he will return one day. The Druze community remained mainly in the mountains of Lebanon and for a period of time came to rule much of Lebanon, part of Syria, Jordan, and Palestine for the Ottoman Sultans. Some Druze communities were established in Palestine and in Jawlan (the Golan Heights) in the seventeenth and eighteenth centuries, but the majority of Druze in Syria's Jabal Druze arrived in the mid 1860s after a conflict between them and the Christian Maronites. They came to dominate the region to such an extent that the mountains once called Jabal al-'Arab became the Jabal Druze.

Little is known about the beliefs of the Druze, who themselves are not generally aware of their faith. In order to help protect themselves from persecution the Druze have developed a hierarchy based on the amount of knowledge the person knows about the religion. Only a small number of the faithful will ever have full knowledge.

THE FIVE PILLARS OF FAITH

All Muslims follow the principles of the religion and adhere to the Five Pillars; the pronouncement of *shahadah* (or declaration of faith), payment of *zakat* (or an alms tax*), siyam* (or fasting during the month of Ramadan), *salat* (or prayer five times a day), and *haj* (or a pilgrimage to Makkah once in their lifetime, if it is financially and physically possible).

Muslims reaffirm their faith by stating the *shahadah* or "there is no god but God and Muhammad is the Prophet of God" on a daily basis. The *shahadah* forms the major part of the call to prayer (or *adhan*), which is heard five times a day before each of the required prayer times. It is also stated when one finishes the required ritual ablution or *wudu'* prior to prayer and is again stated as part of prayer. This strong belief in the unity of God is one of the few major doctrinal differences between Muslims and Christians. Muslims believe that Jesus was a great prophet and accept his virgin birth, but they do not believe that he is the son of God.

Prayer is to be done five times a day by all Muslims. Men are encouraged to pray in a mosque and foster feelings of community. Women may pray in a mosque, but more frequently pray at home. The five times correspond to the movement of the sun and are done at dawn or *fajr,* mid day or *duhur,* mid afternoon or *'asr,* sundown or *maghrib,* and in the evening or *'ishiyah,* which is some two hours after sundown. Many mosques in Jordan offer another prayer at midnight, which is not an obligation, but an act of piety. During the month of Ramadan Muslims offer what is called *tarawih* prayer immediately following the evening prayer. This prayer lasts much longer than the normal one and is an act of piety that marks Ramadan.

Muslims face towards Makkah during prayer as ordered in the Qur'an. Originally Muslims faced towards Jerusalem in recognition of that city's special history of monotheist religion. However, the Prophet was told in a revelation to change the direction to Makkah since it was at Makkah that Ibrahim (Abraham of the Old Testament) was ordered to build the first house for the worship of the one God. Muslims throughout the world face towards Makkah for prayer and finding the correct direction for this is the reason Muslims advanced the sciences in astronomy, geography, and mapping.

Muslims are required to fast during the month of Ramadan from dawn to dusk; from *fajr* to *maghrib*. Fasting means that no food or drink can be consumed during the daylight hours nor can anyone smoke. In fact, nothing should pass the lips during the hours of fasting. The purpose is for all Muslims to understand the hardships that the poor endure all year round, to foster a greater sense of community by everyone being involved in the same activity, and to follow the *Sunnah* of the Prophet Muhammad. Muhammad began a strict regime of fasting before he became the Prophet, and the first revelations of the Qur'an came to him while he was fasting during the month of Ramadan.

Ramadan is a month for reflection and piety. Arguments and disputes are to be avoided, though for those addicted to caffeine and nicotine long days with no coffee or cigarettes often cause ill tempers. When the evening call to prayer is heard, everyone may eat and drink. Following the Ottoman custom, cities like 'Amman use a canon located on the Citadel Hill to announce the fast is over, and in the morning to help announce another day of fasting has begun. The *Sunnah* of the Prophet is to break the fast with dates and milk and then to pray the evening prayer before eating a meal. Many Jordanians follow this practice but perhaps just as many break their fast with a major meal. Ramadan is a time when there are special foods, especially sweets such as *zalabiyah, mushabbak,* and *qatayif. Zalabiyah* is made of light dough poured into a vat of hot oil. The dough is poured into shapes and cooks quickly. When it is taken out of the oil it is covered in a thick, rosewater flavored syrup. When made into rosettes it is called *mushabbak* (or net-like). *Qatayif* is similar to a crepe and is filled with nuts or Turkish delight or ricotta cheese and re-cooked. Again it is covered with thick, rosewater-flavored syrup before being served.

Before the dawn prayer there is another meal called *suhur* during Ramadan. Neighborhoods may hire someone to come around with a drum or trumpet to help wake everyone up so they can eat before the day's fast begins. This person is called the *masaharti*, and in the past children would gather around him to clap and sing as he walked along the streets playing his drum. Today this is not done as much as in the past and instead of a man with a drum, neighborhood teenagers gather to bang on metal pots and pans to wake people up. A canon sounds to note that people should stop eating and another day of fasting has begun.

The 27th day of Ramadan is called Laylat al-Qadir or the Night of Power. It is believed that the first revelations of the Qur'an were given to Muhammad during that night. Laylat al-Qadir is mentioned in the Qur'an and is when the angels descend to earth. Prayers offered during Laylat al-Qadir are believed to be especially important as a result and most Muslim men spend the entire night in the mosque in prayer and contemplation. Jordanian TV covers the night and broadcasts special programs including live coverage from the Ka'abah in Makkah.

Fasting during Ramadan is directly connected to the next pillar, paying the poor tax or *zakat*, which is collected from all Muslims who can afford it. In many Muslim countries today the poor tax is taken out of monthly salaries like any other form of taxation and is administered by a special department within ministries of religious affairs. *Zakat* is not to be used to make a name for the individual donor; it should be donated anonymously and accepted anonymously so that neither party can use it for their own personal benefit. In addition, no one should know how much was given or how much was received but a standard of 10 percent of a person's monthly income is usual.

The fifth pillar is a pilgrimage or *haj* to Makkah once in a person's lifetime. Pilgrimage is not supposed to cause the person doing it any financial or physical difficulties, though many do it whether it will cause them problems or not. For Jordanians the yearly pilgrimage is not as difficult as it is for those traveling long distances such as from Morocco or Indonesia. Public transportation is not that difficult to find nor too costly since Jordan shares a border with Saudi Arabia. In the past the main dangers were from Bedouin raids or in the summer season lack of water. Various Muslim governments organized huge caravans, which passed from Damascus through Jordan, following the ancient trade routes or the Kings Highway, until the sixteenth century when the Ottoman Sultan Sulayman the Magnificent had a new route mapped out called the Young Girls Road or *Tariq al-Bint*. In the early twentieth century this route was followed by the Hijaz Railway and today the modern Desert Highway follows the same route.

ISLAMIC HOLIDAYS

Jordanians celebrate Islamic holidays the most important ones being *'Id al-Fitr* at the end of Ramadan and *'Id al-Adha*, which is held in conjunction with the annual pilgrimage to Makkah. The dates for both of these holidays, like all Muslim holidays, change every year. The Muslim calendar is based on lunar cycles; each month begins with the next new moon meaning that any month can be between 28 to 30 days long. With each passing year, the Islamic month moves approximately two weeks into the solar calendar so that every year the Islamic month starts about two weeks earlier than it did the year before. One Islamic month will have traveled through the entire solar calendar of months every 30 years. The dependence on close observation of the moon is among one of the several ways Islamic societies have contributed heavily to the advancement of astronomy. Since the Islamic calendar is not fixed and depends on the monthly phases of the moon, holidays are officially announced on television the night before.

'Id al-Fitr is also called the 'Id al-Saghir (or Small Feast) and, due to the long period of Turkish domination in Jordan, some of the older people refer to it as Bayram. The few days before the 'Id is a frenzy of shopping for ingredients for the holiday meal and for gifts, especially for children. The 'Id celebration begins with an 'Id prayer in the morning usually held in large mosques, or in large open areas called musallah to allow for large numbers of people followed by a meal, the first day time meal in a month. The meal usually includes ka'k, which is a shortbread sometimes flavored with almond flour made especially for this meal. Children are given gifts, which traditionally were new clothes. Since the arrival of the first cinemas in the Arab world, the holiday is also marked by the release of a new film, often one of the major films for that year. The 'Id al-Fitr holiday period lasts between two to three days depending on whether or not it corresponds to the normal weekend.

'Id al-Adha or Feast of the Sacrifice, also called al-'Id al-Kabir or the Big Feast, is celebrated the 10th day of the Islamic month Dhu al-Haj and marks the conclusion of the haj. The holiday is a yearly re-enactment of Ibrahim's (Abraham of the Old Testament) act of humility and willingness to obey the command of God to sacrifice his first son Isma'il (Ishmael in the Islamic tradition, but Ishaq or Isaac in the Jewish and Christian traditions). God stayed Ibrahim's hand and substituted a lamb for his son. In the Islamic tradition Ibrahim and his son Isma'il then built the first Ka'abah as the first house to the worship of the one God. The strong connection between Ibrahim, his son Isma'l, and his wife Hajar (Hagar) and Makkah is strong. The well of Zamzam is the spring of water that appeared to the desperate Hajar as she ran back and forth trying to find water for Isma'il. This act is also re-enacted by the pilgrims as part of the requirements to complete the pilgrimage.

In Jordan the Turkish name for the holiday Bayram Qurban is also used among the older people. It is expected that every household will buy a sheep, and on the morning of the 'Id the sheep are slaughtered and butchered. Those who can afford to do so may buy several sheep and have them distributed among the poor. Traditionally each family eats part of the lamb on the day of the *Id,* some is dried to be eaten later, and the rest is given to the poor. Today few need to dry the meat and those who do, do so to maintain custom, not because they don't have access to refrigeration.

Another major Islamic holiday is the *Mawlid al-Nabi* (or the Prophet's Birthday) celebrated on the 12th of the Islamic month Rabi' al'-Awwal. The celebration of the Prophet's Birthday is a much newer holiday than *Id al-Fitr* and *Id al-Adha* and dates back to the Fatimid dynasty in Egypt. The Fatimids were the first to officially celebrate the Prophet's Birthday and may have been influenced by the Coptic Christian celebrations for the birth of Jesus. The idea of celebrating the Prophet's Birthday spread from Egypt first to those areas under Egyptian political control. In 1588 the Ottoman Sultan Murad III declared the *Mawlid* an official holiday. Jordanians take the day off, but little else is done to mark the day.

Ashurah is the other major Islamic holiday celebrated on the 10th day of the Islamic month of Muharram. Some scholars have connected the origin of the holiday to the Jewish influences on the early Muslim community in Madinah and to be related to the Jewish Day of Atonement. It is pointed out that at first the day was one of fasting from sunrise to sunset, but later the Prophet, after a revelation, changed the Muslim fast to the month of Ramadan. *Ashurah* corresponds to the death of Imam Hussein, son of 'Ali ibn Abi Talib and grandson of the Prophet Muhammad at Karbala in Iraq in 680. Among Shi'i Muslims it is a day of intense mourning and regret over the death of Imam Hussein at the hands of the Umayyads. For Sunni Muslims the day has become one more for children and is a cross between Halloween's trick or treat and Christmas. Children sing songs and go from house to house where they are given candies and/or money. The holiday is rarely celebrated in its traditional form today and is not taken as a day off from work and school.

CHRISTIANITY IN JORDAN

Christians make up about 20 percent of Jordan's population and of those the vast majority belongs to the Eastern Orthodox Church. As noted before, Christianity is as old as the faith itself in Jordan. One of Christ's miracles recorded in the New Testament took place in the Decapolis city Gadara (Umm Qays today) overlooking the Sea of Galilee. John the Baptist was brought before King Herod at Makawir located near Madaba. In the early years of the religion, Jordan had a flourishing Christian civilization attested by the brilliant mosaics found in places as diverse as Umm al-Risas, Madaba, and Petra. The Christian families from Karak claim direct descent from the Bani Ghassan Arabs who established a kingdom in southern Syria and Jordan in the fifth century.

Eastern and western Christianity began a long process of splitting from each other in the fifth century, which culminated in the final split in 1054 over questions related to the nature of Christ, Mary, and the language of the mass. The Crusader period in the Middle East did little to improve the relationship between the two major divisions of Christianity as the eastern churches suffered under the rule of western rulers and the Byzantine capital, Constantinople, was captured and sacked in the 4th Crusade. Control of holy sites in Jerusalem, Bethlehem, and other locations were placed under western control and were not restored to eastern Christians until the reconquests of Salah al-Din and the Mamluks.

The Eastern Orthodox Church is also divided into a number of different sects though most Jordanians belong to the mainstream branch, which ultimately recognizes the authority of the Patriarch of Constantinople/Istanbul. The Jordanian church has a very strong Arab character, and the Arabic language is used as the official language of the Church. In recent decades the Jordanian Church has been able to gain a degree of local autonomy separating it from control from Jerusalem and having a strong voice in who is selected to lead the community and in the selection of priests. All priests and church officials must be Arabic speaking.

In addition to the Orthodox Christians, there are a number of other smaller Christian groups in the country. The Armenians Orthodox Church is one with a long established presence in the region. The Armenian king converted to Christianity near the end of the third century and Armenia was the first country to be Christianized. The Armenian Church split from most of the rest of Christianity at the Council of Chalcedon in 451, yet has generally kept fairly good relations with the rest of the eastern churches, and shares many of the same tenants of faith with the Egyptian Copts. Historically, the Armenians in Jordan worked as wondering silversmiths in the towns and villages and were connected to larger communities in cities like Damascus and Jerusalem. The majority of Armenians came in 1915 seeking refuge from the Turks after over one million were killed or died of extreme exposure as result of being accused of giving assistance to the Russian army in World War I.

The Catholics are also small in number and most belong to Palestinian communities who once were Eastern Orthodox. Over the centuries certain groups of Eastern Orthodox Christians agreed to place themselves under the Pope, but have been able to keep many of their own practices, including using their own languages for the liturgy.

The Protestants are also mainly Palestinians whose ancestors came under the influence of certain European or American missionaries during the nineteenth and early twentieth centuries. Again, most of the Protestants are descendants of people who converted from Eastern Orthodoxy to one of the many Protestant churches. Most of the Protestants fall under the general control of the Anglican Bishop in 'Amman. Until the 1980s the Protestant community was under the authority of the Anglican Bishop of Jerusalem, but the two were divided to better serve their communities thus the Bishop in 'Amman became the head of the Jordanian Protestants. Among Jordan's small Protestant communities are Lutherans (connected to the German Lutheran Church in Jerusalem), Presbyterians, and Baptists.

Christian Holidays

Eastern churches place far more importance on the crucifixion of Jesus than his birth, and therefore Easter is a far more important holiday than Christmas. Easter is preceded by a 40-day Lenten fast called the Great Lent, and the day itself is celebrated by lengthy masses. Similar to the Muslim holidays, children receive gifts such as new clothes. Following the mass, people have large meals including the food items that had been forbidden during the Lenten fast, such as meat.

The eastern churches have a number of periods of Lenten fasts, and in the total number of days have more fast days of one kind or another than the Muslims. The Lenten periods include: the Great Lent, which falls 40 days before Easter; the Dormition Lent (the Falling Asleep of the Virgin Mary) which lasts 15 days; The Christmas Lent, which is 40 days before Christmas; and 1 day each for the Feast of the Holy Apostles, the day before Epiphany, the Feast of the Beheading of John the Baptist, and the Elevation of the Holy Cross. In addition, Wednesdays and Fridays are Lenten days and, as a result, a large variety of meatless dishes have been developed by eastern Christians. A typical Lenten meal includes cheeses, high protein bean dishes, eggplant, fish, and fruit when in season. Meals to celebrate the end of one of the many Lenten periods usually include a variety of meat and chicken dishes.

Eastern Christmas is celebrated January 7th rather than December 25th. Christmas is less important in eastern Christianity as it is the crucifixion and resurrection of Christ that are more central to the doctrines of the faith. The celebrations for Christmas have become greatly influenced by those of western Christianity, especially with the number of Westerners living in cities like 'Amman and the major hotels all put up Christmas decorations that incorporate Western symbols and images, even Santa Claus and Christmas trees. Western Christmas music, candies, and gifts in colorful wrappings have come to be part of many Christian Jordanians' celebration of the holiday.

In recognition of the fact that there are both western and eastern Christians among its people, Jordan has struck a compromise for public recognition of the holidays. Officially Jordan recognizes western Christmas and eastern Easter as holidays, but each community is allowed to celebrate their own unofficial holidays as well. Banks close for December 25, but government offices remain open. Christian employees are given their own days off, but everyone has their two holidays. In addition to these holidays, Jordanians get Christian and Islamic New Years Day off. While not seen as religious holidays, all citizens are able to enjoy them as holidays.

RELATION BETWEEN THE RELIGIONS

Relation between the different religious communities has generally been fairly good in Jordan. The majority of Jordanians became Muslim within a short period after the initial conquest. Islam is known to have spread into Jordan before the region was under Muslim control, the Ghassanid governor of 'Amman being among the first to convert to Islam. Once the region fell under Islamic government, many of the Christian groups were given more freedom of worship than they experienced under the Byzantines. Priests were no longer required to abide by decisions made by the various councils and enforced by the Byzantine state.

With the opening up of the Syrian Desert to Bedouin tribes from the Peninsula, much of rural Jordan became Muslim. Christianity remained an important religion in towns and cities, such as Damascus and Jerusalem, but more and more of the rural people turned to Islam. Religious reform movements such as the Shi'ite Qaramitah found strong support among the rural Jordanian population and by the eleventh century, Christians were in the minority.

The western Crusaders did little to help the position of eastern Christians whether under their control or in Muslim lands. The numbers of Christians fell in Syria as eastern Christians converted to Islam in order to distance themselves from being identified with the Crusaders. Those who remained Christian asserted their eastern (and Arab) identities. The Mongols who invaded the region in the thirteenth century initially favored the eastern Christians and some of the Mongol elite converted to Nestorian Christianity, but in the end the descendants of the Mongols who settled to rule in the Middle East and Central Asia converted to Islam.

The Ottomans, building on older means of governing, developed a system called the Millet system (from the Arabic word *millah* meaning community), whereby each religious community was responsible for itself to the state. Certain religious leaders came to represent not only their own community but other smaller communities. Most Jordanian Christians were represented by the Patriarch of the Eastern Orthodox Church. Latter, when other communities became recognized, other leaders became responsible for them to the state, such as the Anglican Bishop of Jerusalem. When Jordan became independent, some of these older Ottoman means of dealing with religious minorities remained in effect.

Hostilities between Muslims and Christians have not been a major feature in Jordan's history. Both communities know a good deal about the other, unlike in many other countries where different religious communities remain greatly separated. Certain posts in the government are required to go to Muslims, but in general there is little discrimination based on religion. Christians, especially Palestinians, were once the most educated and westernized part of the population, dominating professions such as medicine and higher education. This gradually changed over the decades after independence, though perhaps Christians still dominate some professions such as medicine.

Recent problems between religious communities in other Middle Eastern countries, such as Lebanon, have not affected relations between Jordanians. Fighting between various militias connected to specific religious communities in Lebanon did not spill over into Jordan. Incidents have been rare and quickly dealt with by the government and by the community leaders. Jordan remains an island of calm in the region.

Jordan's Conservative Society and Popular Religion

Jordanians, whether Muslim or Christian, are conservative. There are social restrictions on the interaction between men and women in the public sphere. Men and women do interact, but within the proper boundaries as set by society. Many Jordanian women are veiled, which means wearing a headscarf, and dressing in clothes that do not reveal much skin. Christians are also conservative, and often it is hard to know religion by the clothes worn.

The conservative nature of the country means that public displays of affection are not appreciated, and the persons involved may suffer consequences at home should the family be made aware. Punishments can be severe, especially for the females who, according to Arab tradition, "wear the family's honor on their skirts." Some Jordanian houses and apartments have been built with two entrances, one for the family to use and one for guests. The one for guests opens up into a special room reserved to receive guests, and they do not need to pass through the part of the house where the family lives. Male guests may or may not see any of the women of the house depending on the closeness of relationship to the family.

Honor plays an important role in society and is the same for Muslims and Christians. Honor is connected with the behavior of individuals and the honor of a family can be ruined by the so-called bad behavior of an individual. The entire family is judged by the actions of an individual, as the actions of the individuals reflect the general moral level of the whole family. While much of this comes from tradition, religion is often used to justify the traditions around values such as honor.

Popular Islam and popular Christianity do not exist in Jordan to the degree that they do in many other Middle Eastern countries. What popular practices exist are localized rather than generalized. A good example of this is the Maqam Shaykh 'Umar al-Malkawi in Malka located in northern Jordan near the Yarmuk River. Shaykh 'Umar al-Malkawi was a pious man who lived in the early sixteenth century. He taught Qur'an and was reputed to be able to cure people of mental illnesses. Of his two sons, people only remember the name of one of them, Ahmad Abu Saqayn. Both are buried next to him. They too were pious men who taught Qur'an and were able to cure people. Ahmad gained the nickname Abu Saqayn (or "He of Two Sets of Legs") because of how quickly he could walk between long distances. The tombs are still visited by those seeking the *barakah* (or "blessings of Shaykh 'Umar and his sons"), but only by those from the nearby villages.

There are several important places associated with Islam, such as the tomb mosque in Mazar of Ja'afar al-Tayir, the brother of 'Ali ibn Abi Talib and a cousin of the Prophet, who was killed at the Battle of Mu'tah in southern Jordan in 630. A number of other Companions of the Prophet are also buried in Jordan; Zayd bin Harithah and 'Abdallah bin Rawahah who fell in the same battle with Ja'afar and are also buried in Mazar, 'Amir ibn Abi Waqqas, and Abi 'Ubaydah 'Amir bin al-Jarrah. Local people do come and offer prayers, but generally they do not ask them to intercede with God.

Jordan has a number of sites connected with both the Old and New Testaments and the Qur'an, such as the tomb of Aaron (Harun) the brother of Moses, 'Ayn Musa (or the Spring of Moses), the tomb of Job (Ayyub) near al-Salt, the tomb of Jethro (Shu'ayb) in Wadi Shu'ayb, and those associated with the Islamic figure known as al-Khidr in Karak, 'Ajlun, Mahis, and Bayt Ras. Again many of these are places where Jordanians come to offer prayers, but generally do not ask for intercession.

Sufism or mystical Islam was never widespread among Jordanians and there are only a few sites associated with Sufi mystics or Sufi brotherhoods. Sufism played a more important role in places such as Damascus and Cairo rather than in Jordan. Those Jordanians attracted to the more mystical dimensions of the religion traditionally have gone to Jerusalem, Damascus, or Cairo to study. Those who were Christians did much the same studying in monasteries in Syria and Lebanon. Thus both Islam and Christianity in Jordan have tended towards the orthodox expressions of the religions.

A practice that is done by both Muslims and Christians is that of making a vow or promise taken at the tomb of an important religious figure or at a religious site. In Greater Syria, which includes Jordan, these are often cross-confessional, meaning that in order for the promise to have greater weight with God, it is taken at a Muslim site by Christians and a Christian site by Muslims. The Eastern Orthodox monastery at Saydniya outside of Damascus is one of the Christian sites used by Muslims, while the tomb of John the Baptist in the Umayyad Mosque in Damascus is one of the Muslim sites used by Christians. On smaller, local levels, the sites associated with the Qur'anic figure al-Khidr are used by both Muslims and Christians. The person making the vow or promise will owe the figure who witnessed it whatever was stated while making the vow: giving a gift of money, clothes, or food for the poor, or giving the first- or second-born child the name of the figure.

Even though mystical forms of both Islam and Christianity have not been popular with Jordanians, it did not negate belief in spirits and magic. A number of ancient archeological sites are believed to be haunted or treasure protected by spirits or *jinn* (genies). One such belief collected in 1986 near the ruins of the Decapolis city Abilah says that the treasure from one of the city's churches, including two golden or gold-covered bells, was hidden in large jars and buried in one of the olive groves. The treasure is protected by a female *jinn* who misdirects those trying to find it. It is possible to be standing on top of the treasure and never see it. Anyone who wants to find the treasure must first find out how to please the *jinn*, who will then reveal the treasure. Local stories collected in the nearby villages of Hartha, al-Khuraybah, and Qarakush say that in the early part of the twentieth century a treasure hunter from the town of Hubras was able to placate the *jinn* and took away one of the two golden bells and sold it Damascus.

Like many others in the Mediterranean region, many Jordanians believe in the evil eye, or more correctly, the eye of envy, *'ayn al-hasud* in Arabic. Admiration of a person, object, or animal will attract the attention of malicious forces and cause harm to the person, object, or animal that is being admired. It is possible to deflect the eye of envy by using certain charms and by always evoking the name of God. When admiring someone or something, one should always say *"Ma Sha' Allah"* meaning "What God Wills." This saying is believed to keep away harm. Children are often protected from harm by charms made from blue glass or by wearing a blue bead. Blue, the color of the eye of envy, helps prevent harm. Lines from the Qur'an, such as the Throne Verse from the second *surah* (or chapter), are frequently used to help prevent the eye of envy from harming a person or object. Jordanian Christians hold the same beliefs and use charms with the Virgin Mary as well as blue beads or blue glass to ward off the eye of envy. Blue beads or religious verses are frequently suspended from the rearview mirrors of cars to help protect against the eye, and trucks may have a doll or a baby shoe suspended from the same mirror to help prevent hitting children. Valuable animals like horses and camels will have blue beads woven into manes, tails, or suspended around their necks. Charms are often hung over the doorways of houses and businesses to help protect the place and those inside it. Practices such as hanging charms in cars or over doorways have become part of tradition, and it does not necessarily mean that the person doing it believes in magic or the ability of the charm to protect the user from harm.

Writing charms or *hijab* is still found in Jordan. Some families are known to have the ability to write effective charms used to ward off evil or to help cure an illness. Those who can write effective charms need to be able to pass on their own *barakah* or blessing to the recipient. Many of those who have this ability claim descent from the family of the Prophet Muhammad, usually through his daughter Fatima and her two sons Hasan and Hussein. Among Christians, some of those who can write charms are priests, while others are ordinary people who have, for one reason or another, been given the ability to write effective charms. Christians have no problem in buying charms from Muslims nor Muslims buying from Christians.

Traditional practices are outside of those accepted by both Islam and Christianity though people often find support for tradition in religion. Jordanians hold to some of them more out of a loyalty to family tradition than to strongly held beliefs, yet popular practices may be resorted to in times of need or trouble. They are familiar and comfortable and do provide mental security when more formal religion may seem too sterile or intellectual.

CONCLUSION

Christian and Muslim Jordanians have a shared history, and culturally there is very little to differentiate one from the other. Few Jordanian towns and villages have or ever had special sections or quarters for the members of any one religion to live, and perhaps this is among the important reasons why many Jordanians have a fair knowledge of the other. When other parts of the Middle East have erupted into sectarian violence there has been very little spillover into Jordan. For example, following the massacres in 1981 by Christian militiamen at the Sabra and Shatilla refugee camps in Lebanon, some young Muslim men had wanted to take revenge on Christians, but the *Imam*s at the mosques spoke against such violence, reminding people of the long-time good relations between the communities in Jordan. Jordan is a conservative Muslim state, but the non-Muslim minorities are not subject to persecution.

3

Literature and Media

The literature and media in Jordan are tied to the wider context of the whole Arab world, where the Arabic language is spoken, that stretches from the Atlantic coast of North Africa to the Persian Gulf. Jordanians do not necessarily see themselves as having a separate and distinct linguistic or literary identity, but see themselves as part of the history of the development of Arabic language, literature, and media. For example, until 1920 most of Jordan was administered from Damascus, the capital of Syria, which has been a major center for Arabic literature since the first centuries of Islam. Being a more rural population until the early twentieth century, much of the local Jordanian literature has historically been oral, but the fact that it has not been written does not mean that it is rustic. Most of the local literature was often in the form of poetry, some of it epic in nature, following the same format as those penned by famous names of Arabic literature in Damascus, Cairo, or Baghdad.

ROLE OF POETRY IN ARAB CULTURE

Arabic as a language has a role in Arab culture that goes beyond that played by most other languages in their cultures. Arabic and the ability to use the Arabic language effectively to create powerful images have a long history stretching back into the pre-literate and pre-Islamic period in the Arabian Peninsula. The development of Classical Arabic as a language is rooted in the literary tradition of the Arab people, and more specifically, the Bedouin, whose spoken dialect eventually became a standard for the language. Classical Arabic is referred to as *Fusha*, which comes from the root meaning clear speech.

The well-rounded man in traditional Arab culture was referred to as an *Adib* meaning someone who was both well mannered and well educated. Being educated meant that he was familiar with literature or *adab,* which also means manners. The idea that the ability to compose literature (both prose and poetry) is linked to good manners and knowledge of how to behave, go back to the pre-Islamic period. All accomplished men were expected to be able to compose poems on any topic at a moment's notice.

During the early historic period in the Arabian Peninsula, the great epic poems composed mainly by Bedouin formed an important basis for both literature and language use. The best of these poems were selected in great contests held annually in Makkah, and the poems of winners were placed in the Ka'abah and, as a result, are referred to as the Suspended Odes or sometimes the Golden Odes. The odes or *qasidah*s followed a set format, which included: opening passages describing an abandoned Bedouin camp, and the happy memories the campsite evokes; an account of a journey across the desert, of the beauty and strength of the poet's horse or camel, and of dangers encountered in the course of his travels; a final passage of a eulogy of a tribe or a particular person or an attack on them, if the poem deals with war or raiding. The odes were originally composed as oral works to be recited where the full body of the Arabic language could be used by the person reciting and felt by the audience listening. Recitations of even well-known ancient works today can cause the audience to respond with deep sighs, loud shouts of approval, or even tears.

These great epic poems recorded the history of the Arabs and much of what is known today about pre-Islamic Arabia comes from studying them. Pre-Islamic period in Arabia is often called *Ayam al-'Arab* or the Days of (meaning the time of) the Arabs (meaning the Bedouin), when tribes fought heroic wars over issues of honor, pasture lands, water, or trade. The poems describe the rise and fall of states, such as that of the Kingdom of Kinda in the ode of its exiled prince Imru al-Qays, tribal wars and feuds, such as the epic of the slave, born 'Antar bin Shaddad, and of the details of tribal life in the desert, such as that of Labib ibn Rabi'a. Even today much of what is known of recent tribal history is recorded only in the poems still recited for the pleasure of the tribe's *shaykh*s, members, or official visitors from the Jordanian government.

Contemporary *qasidah*s composed by Bedouin follow more or less the format as established in great odes, but also make use of contemporary settings and deal with contemporary issues. The poet's fine Arabian horse or Omani camel so vividly described in the older odes are replaced in the modern versions with pickup trucks, four-wheel drive SUVs, and Mercedes-Benz taxis. Political and social comment are still important topics covered by Bedouin poets. Topics for contemporary Bedouin poets include: the wars in Palestine since 1948 or in the Gulf since 1990–91; arrival of refugees from such conflicts; visits to Cairo, Damascus or even European cities; long distance trade or migrant work in the Gulf, Iraq, or other places.

Other forms of poetry have been developed in the Arab world, some in the courts of Damascus, Baghdad, Cairo, Fez, and Cordoba. Among the most widespread is *zajal*. *Zajal* dates to the early period of Arabic literature and became very popular throughout the Arab world due to its use of spoken dialect and the fact that it lent itself easily to music. Composed of rhymed couplets, it also lends itself to improvisation and spontaneity. Bored passengers in a long-distance taxi or bus ride enjoy having someone among them who knows how to make verse and keep them entertained, even if they are the subject of the poet's humor. *Zajal*'s use of couplets and repetition allows the whole audience to participate in the performance, not only just listen to it.

POETRY IN BEDOUIN SOCIETY—VOICE OF THE PEOPLE

Poetry remains the single major literary form composed by Bedouin. Jordan's Bedouin leaders are still entertained, praised, and criticized by their people through poems. Individual tribesmen and women use poems to describe both approval and disapproval of their leaders or family members. Various poetic forms are used from the long epic *qasidah* to short four liners called *rubi'at*. Some of them are sung, such as the *ghinnawi* (or small, short song common among Egyptian Bedouin). The Arab American anthropologist Lila Abu Lughod studied the use of *ghinnawi* by women in particular among the Awlad 'Ali tribe in Egypt's Western Desert as form of political and social comment and protest. Samdar Lavie, an Israeli anthropologist, conducted a similar study of the use of poetry among the 'Azazmah tribe in the Sinai.

Bedouin poetry can be recited or sung, but is more often sung than recited. When the person singing is a man, he often accompanies himself with a one string violin-like instrument called a *rabab*. So closely connected is the *rabab* with poetry that it is often referred to as *rabab al-sha'ir* (or the poet's *rabab*). Singing helps with learning and memorizing older poems and in the composition of new ones. There are a number of forms of sung poetry among the Bedouin depending on the subject matter and length (see the chapter on Music).

CONTEMPORARY JORDANIAN WRITERS

Contemporary Arabic literature began in places like Cairo and Beirut in the second half of the nineteenth century when western forms such as the novel and novella were borrowed, replacing the more classical formats such as the rhymed prose *maqamat*. Arab authors became masters of the novel as a literary form, and the Arab world produced a vast number of novels touching on topics as wide as social justice, effects of war, or less serious subjects for pure entertainment. In poetry contemporary writers have been greatly influenced by free verse breaking the strict regimented rules of classical poetic forms. Contemporary Arabic literature is as vast and varied as any in the world, and has often been one of the few vehicles open to social and political comment and criticism.

Damascus, Baghdad, Beirut, and Cairo are among the major centers for contemporary Arabic literature. Few Jordanians have been well published or recognized outside of their own country until recently. Those Jordanians who have wanted to pursue careers as writers have generally moved to the major centers in the Middle East or even to Europe or North America. Most of their writings are in Arabic and until the 1990s little of it was available in English translation. Thanks to the efforts by such people as Dr. Salma Jayyusi and the Project of Translation from Arabic Literature or PROTA Jordanian (and other Arab authors) are now accessible to the English language reader.

One of the first Jordanian authors to be translated into English is Ibrahim Nasrallah. Like many Jordanian writers, he is of Palestinian origin, though has lived most of his life in 'Amman. Nasrallah first made a name for himself as a poet, and he is well-known and appreciated in much of the Arab world. His novel *Prairies of Fever*, written between 1977 and 1983, draws heavily on his own personal experience working in Saudi Arabia, and it deals with issues of identity. The main character, Muhammad Hamad, struggles in his attempt to maintain his own identity amongst the bleak place where he is employed to teach school. The novel is a masterpiece of postmodern Arabic literary style—a definite break with the forms of classical Arabic literature—showing the influences of Egyptian novelists such as the daring Yusuf al-Qa'id.

Ghalib Halasa is another of the early Jordanian pioneers of modern literary forms. Born in 1932 Halasa wrote seven novels and two collections of short stories before his death in 1989. His strong pro-Palestinian political activities caused him to "lead an interrupted life," according to Denys Johnson-Davies. He lived in a number of Arab capitals during his life, including Beirut, Damascus, Baghdad, and Cairo. He was expelled from Egypt in 1976 as a result of his politics. His writings reflect his own life and are set in a number of different Arab countries such as Egypt.

Liyana Badr is of Palestinian origin. Born in Jerusalem, her life has been described as a "series of exiles," first from Palestine to Jordan in 1948, then from Jordan to Lebanon in 1970 as a result of the Black September conflict between the Jordanian army and the Palestinian fighters, and eventually to

Tunisia. *A Balcony over the Fakihani* is a set of novellas that explore the life of Palestinians living in exile (in Jordan and Lebanon) as well as accounts of the 1982 Israeli invasion of Lebanon. While Badr gives the reader an excellent and personal description of the lives of Palestinian exiles, Sahar Khalifeh, another Palestinian Jordanian author, gives a vivid account of life under Israeli occupation of the West Bank in her novel *Wild Thorns.* In this novel Khalifeh discusses the collapse of the traditional family system under the strain of the Israeli occupation: problems of honor; the emerging role of women; and the conflict between political idealism and the harsh realities of life under occupation.

While most Jordanian and Palestinian writers have produced their works in Arabic, the Jordanian writer Fadia Faqir's novel *Pillars of Salt* was written in English. Faqir is of Bedouin origin and pursued a career in creative writing in the United Kingdom where she now lives and works, teaching Arabic literature at the University of Durham. Both of her novels, *Nisanit* and *Pillars of Salt,* were written in English and published by Western presses. *Pillars of Salt* explores the lives of two Jordanian women through their own narrations of their life histories. While set in the 1940s and 1950s, the lives of the two women can be seen as typical of many Jordanian women who are struggling against the patriarchal nature of their society limiting what women are allowed to do.

The Bedouin poet Muhammad Fadil al-Hajaya uses more traditional poetic styles to express his political views. Following the conventions of Bedouin poetry, he has produced a number of *qasidahs* critical of American foreign policy and the actions of Arab governments. His poems *O Condoleza Rice* and *Fad'as and Fad'us* (names used by Jordanian Bedouin for the rulers of the Gulf States under U.S. protection) were widely distributed in Jordan. His fame is growing and his poems were discovered by Said Abu Athera and Clive Holes, who have provided the first English translations of his verse.

MEDIA IN JORDAN

Media in Jordan consists of both print and nonprint varieties. Print media are primarily newspapers and journals, while the nonprint media are primarily radio and television. Most of the media are controlled by the state, either directly as state organizations, such as television, or through state censorship. With the growth of satellite television and the availability of media from other Arab and non-Arab countries, state control over Jordanian media has had to adjust. Generally speaking, even with state control over the major forms of media, information on a wide range of topics is available, and people are fairly free to voice their personal opinions. In 2003 major changes were made to Jordanian laws that have opened up the media to more critical reporting and analysis of news events, even allowing criticism of the King. Despite these changes, the media-rights organization, Reporters Without Borders, has noted that the government still sets the tone for most of the media coverage of news. The official news agency called Petra is state run by the Ministry of Information.

Print media published in Jordan are mainly state controlled. There are four daily Arabic language newspapers, one daily English language newspaper, and one weekly English language newspaper. Of the Arabic newspaper, *al-Dustur* (or *The Constitution*) is one of the most widely read with *al-Ra'i* (or *The Opinion*) following in second place. These two Arabic papers and the English language *Jordan Times* are the most important source of print news, and though more or less free to print what they want, they remain cautious in their editorials. It will take some time for the local journalists to feel the new laws will protect them from the state. All of the major print media are published in 'Amman while other less widespread newsletters and newspapers are published in regional cities.

Newspapers have an important role in the mainly male coffeehouse culture of Jordan. Reading the newspapers, frequently a number of different ones, over cups of Turkish coffee or Arab tea are how many Jordanian men begin their day. Once the newspapers are read, noting differences in coverage and tone, Jordanian men are ready for one of their main passions, political discussions with friends. Years of state censorship has only served to refine reading between the lines and develop a keen sense of political discourse.

An equally important source of news and entertainment is the state-controlled radio and television company, called Radio Television Jordan. Jordanian television has four channels; Channel One is primarily in Arabic; Channel Two broadcasts films; Channel Three, which some call the "Foreign Channel," has a number British or American programs with Arabic subtitles; and the Jordanian Satellite Channel. The Jordanian Satellite Channel is broadcast to the greater Arab world and to Arabs living in Europe, North America, and to other places with sizable Arab immigrant communities such as Australia. Jordan's satellite channel has to compete with the large array of other satellite channels now available and has made attempts to have a broader appeal than to only Jordanian and Palestinian immigrant communities, such as including hard-hitting news programs and a variety of entertainment programs.

Jordanian television has also had a long history of Hebrew language news broadcasts aimed at Israelis in response to the Arabic news broadcasts on Israeli television, which are easily picked up in Jordan without needing an extra antenna. Depending on where one is living in Jordan, it has been possible to have a variety of television viewing long before the arrival of satellite channels. It has been easy for Jordanians to watch Egyptian, Saudi, Syrian, Iraqi, Lebanese, Israeli, and even Cypriot television since the late 1960s and early 1970s. Access to the wider world via television has given the Jordanian viewer a sophisticated sense of choice and an ability to sift through what is broadcast as news. The competition has also had a role in developing better quality Jordanian television programming.

Radio, for the most part, is also operated by the government as part of Radio Television Jordan. The radio services are in Arabic, English, and French and include a wide variety of programs. Among the popular formats are caller programs where listeners are encouraged to call in and engage in frank discussion. Usually called Direct Contact or *Bath Mubashir,* these programs give the people a forum to complain about state services or even specific ministries or ministers. In addition to the state radio station there has been a growth of private radio stations, but they tend to be entertainment oriented and play popular music. The Jordanian armed forces also operate its own radio station, which includes news and entertainment.

FILM AND *MUSALSALAT*

Jordan does not have a film industry; major Arabic language film making in the region is done in Egypt and Syria. Egyptian and Syrian films are broadcast on Jordanian television and shown in cinemas where they are among the most popular films viewed by local people. Hollywood has made several major films in Jordan, the best known being *Lawrence of Arabia* and the last of the Indiana Jones's series *Indiana Jones and the Last Crusade.* Jordan has not been able to compete with other Arab countries, such as Morocco, as a locale for Hollywood films mainly because Jordan is much more expensive as a location.

Jordan does produce a number of Arabic soap operas or *musalsalat.* In the 1970s Jordan began specializing in "Bedouin soap operas," which they quickly came to dominate. Using outdoor sets, the Jordanian Bedouin soaps used as many authentic props as possible, from tents and tent furnishings to live animals. Jordanian actors' ability to speak with a Bedouin accent made these types of series more appealing, because they sound more or less correct to the viewers. In order to have a broader appeal outside of Jordan, the actors developed a generic Bedouin dialect using features from a number of Bedouin dialects found throughout the Arabian Peninsula. Thus the Jordanian Bedouin soaps are eagerly purchased by television stations in Saudi Arabia, the Gulf States, and Iraq. Jordan's only real rival in producing Bedouin series comes from Syria, but in recent years more and more such series are joint productions, including financial backing from the Arab Gulf States and technical and dramatic expertise from both Jordan and Syria.

A second type of television series that are somewhat like the Bedouin soaps revolve around rural or village life. These are frequently set in the period before World War II or soon afterwards—no specific dates are usually mentioned—and deal with traditional village life. The productions are usually filmed in some of the better-preserved Ottoman-period sites in the country adding to their authenticity. Themes in these series center on the changes from traditional patriarchy and strict codes of conduct for especially the women of the household, to more progressive attitudes about women's education and employment without the loss of family honor. Others deal with the sensitive issue of honor crimes, where a girl may be killed by her male relatives for injuring family honor. Family honor can be compromised should a girl have relationships, even friendships, with men outside of the circle of her close male relatives. Jordan is one of the few countries in the region that is actively confronting the issue of honor crimes and the state uses television as a vehicle for discussion.

In addition to Bedouin and rural soaps, Jordan also produces a number of excellent quality historical dramas. Again, since the 1990s many of these are joint Gulf/Syrian/Jordanian productions, and some of them, such as the 2003 series on the life of the pre-Islamic poet prince Imru al-Qays, are filmed in Morocco. The topics of many of these are bold and new, such as the Syrian-Jordanian series called *Tariq illa Kabul* or *The Road to Kabul* about the Soviet invasion of Afghanistan, the subsequent rise of the Taliban, and their eventual fall during the American invasion. The story was personalized through one Afghan family and the choices its members made, such as the daughter who studied Western medicine in Britain and the son who joins the Taliban in Pakistan. The series included Jordanian and Syrian actors and was filmed nearly entirely in southern Jordan.

Jordanian television produces a number of series primarily aimed at the Jordanian viewing audience as well. These are often set in 'Amman and deal with current social and political issues in the country such as the impact of war in the region, education, unemployment, and changes in the family structure due to life in the big city. Again the use of outdoor sets and the high quality of acting distinguish the Jordanian-made programs from those produced in Egypt. Egyptian soaps are still extremely popular with the viewing audience but are seen as too canned, many having more or less the same topics and ending the same way. Since the 1980s, both Jordanian and Syrian series have been able to compete very well with those made in Egypt. Syrian series often tackle topics simply not dealt with by any other Arab country, including homosexuality, AIDS, and other such sensitive issues. Jordanian productions are usually not as bold in dealing with such topics, but do tackle important and difficult political topics such as government corruption, the economic impact of globalization, and the growth of democracy in the region. Such topics may not be dealt with directly, but through the lens of historical dramas where characters from the Arab past speak of them.

CONCLUSION

The impact of Jordan's literature and media is primarily the result of its nonprint media. Jordanian television, through its satellite channel and through its made for television dramas, has made important contributions to the development of contemporary Arab language media. The high quality of its actors, production techniques, and interesting story lines have made Jordanian made for television programs among the most influential in the Arab world. Jordanians have also assisted or worked as full partners in all stages of production with Syrians, Moroccans, and other Arabs creating new and challenging commentaries and criticisms of contemporary Arab society.

4
Architecture, Art, and Traditional Crafts

Architecture, art, and traditional crafts in Jordan are linked to the history of the country and its religious and ethnic diversity. Jordan has a rich archeological heritage stretching back into antiquity, which has influenced subsequent architectural designs and elements of decoration. Jordanian crafts, such as pottery and work in silver, are also closely tied to the long history of the region, or to specific ethnic groups such as the Circassians.

BEDOUIN ARCHITECTURE—THE HOUSE OF HAIR

It is appropriate to begin the discussion of Jordanian architecture with the Bedouin tent. The nomad tent is an ancient aspect of architecture not only in Jordan but the entire region stretching from the deserts of North Africa to those of Central Asia. Bedouin call their tent *bayt sha'r* (or house of hair) to distinguish it from the permanent homes constructed by villagers that the Bedouin call *bayt hajar* (or house of stone).

The tent used by Bedouin in Jordan is similar to those found in the Arabian Peninsula, parts of Iran, Turkey, and Egypt but differs in shape and even in the materials used from those developed for the different climates in much of the North African Sahara or those in Central Asia. The nomad tent in Jordan is made from woven panels of black goat hair, which gives the tent the ability to be warm and water-resistant during the wet, winter months and cool and dry during the hot summer season. Goat hair, unlike wool, is hollow and when it rains the hair fills with moisture causing it to swell making it the best possible construction material. Once filled with moisture, the hair is naturally water-resistant and the rain runs off of it. The hair is also light, even when filled with water, compared to wool, which when wet becomes too heavy for the wood poles and rope ties to bear and a tent made from it will collapse. The hair also allows air to circulate in the hot, dry summers and helping cool the interior of the tent even during the heat of the day. Another advantage of using hair instead of wool is that it is much easier to fold up and transport, especially in the past when camels were used.

Tents are made of a number of strips of woven goat hair which are usually about 60 to 80 centimeters or 2 to 2.5 feet wide. New replacement panels are added to the front of the tent while older panels that are showing strain from years of use are used along the lower part of the back wall. Often on the very bottom or the *safalah,* where the tent touches the ground, pieces of cheap, low-quality, easily replaced sack cloth are used. Old tent panels with too many holes or tears are cut up and made into useful items such as bags while that which can not be reused is thrown away. The whole structure—the roof or *shagag,* the back wall or *ruwag,* front wall or *sitar,* and the side walls or *ruf-fah*—are joined together by using sharp wooden pins called *khilal.* The front and back walls usually have a middle panel made of both black goat hair and white wool for decoration. The two or three pole tents used by most families are usually around 2 meters or over 6 feet tall, between 9 to 16 meters or 27 to 48 feet long, and between 3.5 to 4.5 meters or 10.5 to 13.5 feet wide.

The Jordanian Bedouin tents come in a number of different sizes from very small one pole tents to massive structures with eight poles or more used by Bedouin leaders to entertain guest and hold tribal councils. Tents are named according to the number of middle poles or *wasat* needed to hold up the roof—side poles are never counted. Small one pole tents called *gatbah* are used by families when on the move or when there is no need to divide the structure into private, family quarters and open, public quarters. Generally speaking most tents are the two pole type called *fazah* or *wasatayn* or the three pole type called *mthawlath.*

Tents are divided into two main sections by a highly decorated wool curtain called a *sahah* in Jordan. The *sahah* shows the weaving talents of the women of the household, and are, like the whole tent structure itself, made on a narrow ground loom, and the panels have to be sewn together once they are all finished. There are a number of different decorative traditions used by Bedouin women when making a *sahah,* which involve using two major methods of weaving, *ragm* or warp patterns and *nagash* or twined weft patterns. The more common warp patterns run the entire length of the piece and women use natural white or brightly dyed wool yarn to make the designs.

The dividing curtain separates the tent into two major living spaces: one for the family and not open to visitors, which is usually called *al-mahram* (or the family or women's side of the tent); and the other section used to host visitors and guests, which is usually called *al-shigg* (or the public or men's side of the tent). Both sections have their own hearth, the one in the public side is used mainly to keep tea and coffee available for guests. Women are able to go back and forth between the two sections and join in the conversations either by interjecting from across the *sahah* or by coming to the public side and sitting with the guests. While Bedouin women have the ability to move back and forth between the two sections of a tent, men do not. Only males from the household or close male relatives of the women may join them on their side of the tent. Conversations between the women, though they may be overheard by men on their side of the curtain, are not heard, while women have no such social customs to prevent them from hearing what is going on in the public section of the tent.

The women's section is where most of the domestic tasks take place and include the family's sleeping quarters. The arrangement of the space reflects the work needs of the women, for example sleeping materials and anything not needed immediately for a task are neatly folded up and either stacked in a pile against the back and side walls or suspended in large bags hung from the tent poles out of the women's way. When something is needed, it is quickly brought from its place and returned when no longer in use. The hearth is used to cook the family's food but does not need to be kept going all day like the one for tea and coffee in the public section.

Village Architecture—the House of Stone

Jordanian village architecture dates as far back as the first permanent structures ever built by man in the Neolithic period (8000 B.C.). Some of the oldest and most important early settlement sites in the Middle East are found in Jordan such as Baydah (just north of Petra), 'Ayn al-Ghazal ('Amman), and Tell al-Sultan (Jericho). These early settlements were built of stone often with the shared walls between houses for greater stability. They were built close to important water sources and near their fields of wheat or on the top of hills to provide better protection from possible attack. The integration of house and protective structures for livestock are features that have survived into the present times in many rural villages not only in Jordan, but around the world.

Some of Jordan's villages have been lived in for millennia. Archeological excavations have been able to prove long term use that stretches back to at least the Iron Age (1200 B.C.), if not earlier, for many Jordanian towns and villages. Some are mentioned by name in the famous Tell Amarna correspondence (1352–1333 B.C.). These are letters between the many princes ruling the small states in Jordan and Palestine to the Egyptian Pharaoh Akhenaten

(1353–1335 B.C.). Other ancient cities in Jordan were founded by veterans from Alexander the Great's armies and they introduced features of Greek urban life, such as the agora, straight column-lined streets, and places for public entertainment such as amphitheaters and hippodromes. Though the Hellenistic and Roman periods in Jordan lasted well over 700 years, they had little lasting influence on the architecture of the country. The most lasting influence came with the arrival of Islam and the blending of ancient Middle Eastern, Greco-Roman, and Arab Islamic features.

Most typical traditional village homes are square structures rarely more than one story tall. They have no or few windows and one front entrance, which opens up to an area that divides the house into public and private halves, not unlike the division in a Bedouin tent. The public area is often to the right of the person when entering the door and the private, family side is located to the back and left. The back is where the kitchen is found, and the back door opens up to a small courtyard or *hosh* that is often at least partially paved with flagstones or cement where much of the women's work is done. The courtyard often has one or more fruit (mulberry, orange, etc.) or nut trees (almonds) that provide important shade in the summer as well as produce for the family. Further shade is provided by a low-roofed over-area called a *ma'rrash*. In many homes the traditional bread oven or *tabun* is located in the yard as well. The ovens are built using a clay and straw mixture and lined with small stone pebbles to hold the bread as it bakes. The uncooked bread is slapped against the stones and is rapidly baked, the fire cooking it on one side and the hot stones cooking it on the other. The fuel is added underneath the oven through a special opening. The whole oven is housed in a small one-room building. In many villages each quarter would have one such oven that served as place where women could meet and talk, much like a village guesthouse for men.

The family room, similar to the Bedouin tent, has bedding, clothes, and the like neatly stacked against the wall when not in use or needed. The floors are covered with rugs often made on the same type of ground loom used by Bedouin women while the walls are hung with Qur'anic passages (or from the New Testament if the family is Christian) often made in embroidered cross-stitch by women of the family. Paint on glass pictures made in Damascus again depicting religious scenes or the pilgrimage caravan were very popular, but have been replaced in recent years with wall clocks or commercially produced calligraphy.

The public room is used to entertain guests and can be quickly converted into a guest bedroom if the visitors stay overnight. The public room is similar in construction to the family's room and is furnished in a similar fashion with mats, rugs, and pillows, and today often with a television. In older homes there may be a place for a hearth in the center of the room to prepare tea and coffee, but generally speaking the tea and coffee are prepared in the kitchen, and children are dispatched to bring it to the host and his guests.

In some villages there are large mansions built by local notables and tribal leaders. These massive homes are traditionally located physically higher up a hill than those of the lesser village families and thus referred to as the Upper or *Fawqah* quarter while the rest of the villagers live in the Lower or *Tahtah* quarter. The massive homes are called throne houses or *Dar al-Kursi* in reference to the special room used to entertain guests located on the second floor. The great houses often have massive front entrances and may be the only ones in a village that use urban architectural decorative motifs from those found in cities like Damascus. Some of the houses have dedications inscribed above the door stating the name of the first of the family to build the house and the date the house was built. The al-Rusan family house in the village of Umm Qays in northern Jordan has such a dedication stone that states the house was built in 1898 by Falah al-Rusan, who was the local military leader or *qa'id* for al-Saru *nahiyah* (district) and the mayor or *mukhtar* of Umm Qays. The entrances to these throne houses are usually flanked by stone benches called *mastabah*s where those who came to see the head of household may be asked to wait. The massive entrances open up to large courtyards, which often have their own well and again fruit or nut trees to help provide shade. The various rooms of the houses open up onto the courtyards, and in the largest of these houses, a second smaller courtyard may also be found for the private use of the women of the family in imitation of the big homes of the urban elite in Damascus, Aleppo, and Baghdad.

Guests are ushered to a large, square room overlooking the entrance. The elevation and tall, narrow windows allow breezes to blow through and cool the room in the summer. The windows of homes belonging to the wealthier and more powerful of the families are glassed with wooded shutters that can be closed in the winter to keep it warm. Guests can be entertained yet be somewhat isolated from the daily activities of the family. The room is usually well-furnished with the best quality carpets from Anatolia, Iran, or Egypt; the pillows and mats are covered with fine cloth from urban centers such as Damascus, Homs, and Aleppo. The brass brazier placed in the middle of the room and other brass and copper furnishings are kept well-polished and bright. The quality of the room and the lavish hospitality served by the host was all part of honor and reputation among the rural elite in the past, and is preserved to a great extent today.

The most elaborate of these throne houses were built in the late Ottoman period. The late Ottoman style included the use of tall windows (nearly floor to ceiling), usually in pairs. The windows were glassed and the most expensive would be made with colored glass in geometric patterns that would cast colored shadows in the room. Syrian mirrors, chests, cabinets, and other furniture made of wood inlayed with mother-of-pearl were highly popular. Some of the larger pieces of furniture were so covered with mother-of-pearl that they are completely encrusted with it. This type of furniture is no longer popular with the rural elite and most of them have now been sold to antique dealers in 'Amman, Damascus, and Aleppo.

Today newer village homes are constructed with cement rather than with stone. Cement is cheaper and easier to build with, though not as good for the climate, which is cold in the winter and hot in the summer. However, it is easier to expand cement houses, and often the builder slowly expands it as the family grows in size or as they are able to afford it. Reinforced metal rods are left exposed indicating plans for future expansion. Cement homes tend to follow the same building plan as the older, traditional stone houses, but include more contemporary features such as indoor plumbing and bathrooms. Kitchens might be larger than the older ones and most homes no longer include the traditional bread oven or *tabun*. In a survey of one in three northern villages conducted in the late 1980s, only one family was found to still maintain a traditional bread oven and only because they liked the taste of the bread baked in it. The family was not poor and the traditional bread oven was maintained because they wanted to, not because they needed to.

Urban Architecture—The Ottoman Legacy

Though many of Jordan's cities have ancient origins, the most noticeable legacy today is that of the late Ottoman period corresponding to the time when Ottoman authority was expanding in Jordan (1840 to 1917). A few cities such as al-Salt and Karak have maintained a significant Ottoman core of both residential and commercial areas. Unfortunately, in most of Jordan many of the Ottoman buildings have been torn down and replaced with more modern ones, especially during the late 1960s and into the 1970s. What is left of the Ottoman period is now being given greater value as an important part of Jordan's cultural heritage and there are efforts to preserve it.

Ottoman buildings can be classified into several regional styles. In northern Jordan, where it is possible to use both white or off-yellow limestone and black basalt, the building often are made with alternating rows of the different-colored stone called *ablaq*. While this use of stone is older than the Ottoman period, being a feature of urban Mamluk architecture and much older as a rural style in southern Syria, it was used in building several important public structures in Irbid, for example. The Ashrafiyah Mosque in 'Amman, though built in the post-independence period maintains an Ottoman floor plan with a large-domed prayer hall, is the only building in 'Amman built with the alternating rows of limestone and basalt.

The majority of Jordan's Ottoman buildings are noted for their elegant but simple façades. Late Ottoman features such as narrow, tall windows are on the second floor, while the street level only has the door. The street level is used for livestock such as riding or carriage horses or for storage. Once in the doorway, the person goes up a narrow staircase to the second floor where the family lives. Most of the buildings are not more than two stories tall, though a few may have a third. The limestone mellows with age and slowly turns to an off-yellow or a soft-gray color. Jordan's urban elite were not as wealthy as those in Damascus or Cairo, and there are none of the major buildings, public or private, as there are in the major cities of the empire.

Recently the Jordanian public has begun to reassess the Ottoman period of their history, and some of the buildings have been purchased to be converted into restaurants or even holiday centers. One farmstead on the southern fringe of 'Amman has been turned into a theme village called *Kan Zaman* (or Once Upon a Time). It includes a number of shops selling traditional crafts, a traditional coffeehouse, and a restaurant that features Jordanian, Palestinian, and Syrian foods. The same developer has opened another such restored village in the south of the country, not far from Petra, called *Taybah Zaman* (or Once Upon a Time in Taybah), which was the name of the village before it was abandoned in the 1970s. Similar to *Kan Zaman, Taybah Zaman* offers the visitor a look into late Ottoman Jordan through shops, coffeehouses, and restaurants, and the chance to spend the night in one of the restored houses.

Contemporary Urban Architecture in Stone

Contemporary Jordanian urban architecture has pushed the limits of what is possible in stone construction. Jordanian architects have used local limestone as the main construction material, or used it to face mainly cement structures. Limestone and limestone-faced buildings give 'Amman and other Jordanian cities a soft mellow look even in the harsh midday summer sun. Structures built from the 1940s to the 1960s oftentimes use more traditional floor plans and some maintain the late Ottoman-styled windows. In general, most of the buildings from this time period do not exceed five stories.

Starting in the 1970s 'Amman in particular had an explosion in the construction sector and middle-class Jordanians were willing to be more bold in the designs of their homes. Not only were architects given the chance to explore the limits of limestone in designs, but ideas were brought in from a wide variety of sources including the neo-classical ante-bellum style from the American south. Rather than the usual squared-off plans of the more traditional stone buildings, architects began designing buildings with rounded corners, spirals, half circles, A-frame or other types of sloping roofs, and a wide range of window types and sizes. The buildings often combine features from a variety of origins, making 'Amman a post-modern city, before post-modern was a term.

More recent buildings have combined cement with stone making them affordable, but able to be much larger than what was possible in stone alone. The most striking of the modern buildings is the King 'Abdallah I Mosque dedicated in 1989. The mosque is constructed of cement but the octagonal floor plan for the prayer hall takes its inspiration from the Dome of the Rock in Jerusalem. The main prayer hall is covered in a massive dome covered in mainly blue tile. The minarets, also made of cement, have a sculpted look as if made of some soft material and shaped with a knife or fork. The mosque has become a major landmark in the city and a symbol of the new architectural styles, exhibiting both a break from and a continuation of older building styles.

Palestinian Refugee Camps

Any discussion of architecture and housing in Jordan has to include Palestinian refugee camps. Jordan has a number of major camps located mainly in the Jordan valley and in and around the cities of 'Amman, Jarash, and Irbid. The camps were set up after the 1948 Arab-Israeli War for the thousands of displaced Palestinians and were augmented in the aftermath of the 1967 Arab-Israeli War when many Palestinian refugees were made refugees for the second time. The camps were originally tent cities, but with time the tents were replaced with semi-permanent housing in most of the camps, or with permanent buildings in those located within the city of 'Amman.

One of the main features of the camps, even those now turned into urban neighborhoods, is the close, dense space. Buildings in traditional neighborhoods and villages are usually not crowded and are allowed a degree of space, especially in villages. The Palestinians were used to similar special arrangements in their home villages, but the need to house large numbers helped create the more crowded conditions found yet today. Between 1948 and 1967, a number of the camps, first established in 'Amman, were converted by the Palestinians into urban neighborhoods and temporary housing was replaced with permanent stone or stone and cement structures. It was difficult to identify the former camps from other working-class neighborhoods in the city other than by their more crowded nature. Urban renewal schemes starting in the 1980s removed several of these neighborhoods, which have now been replaced with major a network of roads.

Most of the Palestinian neighborhoods in ʻAmman have been absorbed into the city but those located outside of the city, such as the huge Biqaʻ Camp, are still noticeable. The Biqaʻ Camp is one of the largest in the country and most of the people have found work in the commercial agricultural farms nearby. The camp is extremely dense with a network of narrow alleys running through it, rather than real roads. The housing is semipermanent, that is while the walls may be made from cement, the roofs are metal panels held in place by cement bricks and rocks. The reason for this is that most of the Palestinians do not want to be permanently settled in the camps, even if they have been refugees since 1948, rather they want to have the right to return to their homes in Palestine. The lack of certain services and the semi-permanence of their homes give them the feeling that living in the camps is a temporary condition.

Circassian Architecture—Caucasus in the Desert

Circassian and Shishan (Chechen) refugees began to arrive in Jordan in the second half of the nineteenth century. After the defeat of their main leader, Shaykh Shamil, at the hands of the Russians, many Circassian and Shishan families fled to Ottoman territory. The Ottomans were in the process of expanding their rule over the more fringe areas of Syria and Jordan and began settling them where they could help maintain order and protect the cultivated areas from Bedouin raids. The Ottoman authorities helped them settle Jarash, Wadi al-Sir, Suwaylah, Naʻur, and al-Azraq. The Circassians and Shishans brought with them their methods of building, using wood and stone, and their style of architecture influenced by the mountain environment of their homeland.

A few buildings in Circassian style still remain in the older part of Jarash and Wadi al-Sir, but the majority of them, like most of the Ottoman period buildings, have been torn down and replaced with newer, cement structures. The few that do remain are distinctive with the use of pitched roofs rather than the local flat style. The roofs are tiled, often in green or red roofing tiles. There is more use of wood in the structure of the roofs and ceilings, setting them off from the local building methods.

Traditional Arts and Handicrafts

Jordan's traditional arts and handicrafts reflect the fact that the country has been a region of small towns, villages, and pastoral nomads since the last centuries of Roman and Byzantine rule (fifth to seventh centuries A.D.). Most of the arts and handicrafts were made for use, for work, and were made from local natural resources: wool, goat or camel hair; olive, citrus, or oak wood; straw; and clay. Most of the items were homemade and were primarily the work of women. A small professional class of male artisans lived and worked in cities such as Karak, Jarash, al-Salt, 'Ajlun, and Irbid or traveled among the villages and Bedouin camps setting up makeshift workshops to make or repair items. The finer quality items were made by master craftsmen in Damascus, Homs, Aleppo, Musil, Baghdad, or Cairo. Some Palestinian cities such as Jerusalem, Hebron, al-Majdal, and Gaza were also well-known for their pottery, woodwork, or cloth, which were marketed to Jordanians. Wealthier Jordanian families displayed their wealth by furnishing their homes with imported items from these urban centers.

ART IN WOOL—BEDOUIN ART OF WEAVING

Perhaps the most representational Jordanian craft is Bedouin weaving. Bedouin women weave a wide variety of items, everything from tent panels to small bags, on ground looms. Ground looms are simple constructions but, because the warp is permanently fixed, the weaver must physically move the shed and separate the warp threads to create the needed countershed to make a woven item. She has to do this every time the shed and countershed have to be created, and because the warp is often made of goat hair, the process is even harder since goat hair is sticky and the threads are hard to separate. The loom itself is narrow, only about 60 to 80 centimeters or about 2 to 2.5 feet wide, and all items woven on it are narrow or are made in strips and sewn together usually using the herring bone or *habak* stitch.

There are two major types of pattern weaving done on a ground loom, warp patterns or *ragm* and twined weft weave or *nagash*. *Ragm,* the name coming from the Arabic word for numbers, patterns are made by using different colored warp threads that run lengthwise along the piece. The weaver selects the one thread needed for the color and pattern on the face of the piece, and the other threads are left loose on the back side to be used only when those colors are needed in the pattern. *Ragm* items have a definite front and back with the back having loose threads the whole length of the pattern on the face.

Nagash, the name coming from the Arabic word for engraving, patterns are more difficult to make and involved a technique used in making tapestries. The weaver uses two weft threads that she wraps two or three times around the warp threads making the design. The method often leaves slits between some of the warp threads as is done in slit tapestries, but the Bedouin weaver seldom leaves long slits and instead brings the pattern together by using overlapping designs such as diamonds. Unlike the *ragm* designs that can only run lengthwise, *nagash* patterns run the width of the piece and skilled weavers can make them match when the strips are sewn together in the end. With *nagash* weave pieces both sides are fronts, as the design is found on both sides since the weft threads are wrapped around the warp threads to make the patterns.

Ground loom weaving is not an art form of Bedouin women only, but village women may also be skilled in making rugs and bags on the same type of loom; however, Bedouin women are without a doubt the masters of this craft. With few tools Bedouin women card, spin, and weave wool and hair produced by their own livestock into works of art. Wool is taken to cities or villages to be dyed into bright reds, oranges, yellows or dark blues and greens; few Bedouin women dye their own yarn. Bedouin women who are skilled weavers are valued members of their community and today are important sources of family income. The art of weaving has been revived in Jordan since the 1980s both as individual response by Bedouin women to demands by tourists, and also through development programs such as the Bani Hamida Project where Bedouin women are encouraged to make items that better fit contemporary European and American houses both in size and in color. The Bani Hamida Project is highly successful in providing Bedouin women with opportunities to provide income from their traditional skills.

In addition to the items produced on ground looms, Jordan's traditional crafts include items made on vertical looms. Vertical looms can be built both indoors or outside and, as the name implies, the loom is constructed vertically sometimes with movable parts. They are more comfortable for the weaver as it is possible to sit while working and it is not necessary to bend over or to physically separate the warp threads to make the shed and countershed operations. Vertical looms are more frequently found in villages where it is possible to build a loom frame on a more permanent basis than is possible for Bedouin women. Vertical looms are not only women's tools, but men's as well. In some villages in Jordan and Syria, men used to weave Bedouin tent panels on vertical looms, which they sold directly to Bedouin or marketed through urban merchants in cities such as Damascus or 'Amman.

Madaba and Karak are famous in Jordan for fine rugs and cloth made on horizontal treadle looms. Treadle looms, unlike the ground and vertical looms, are a male domain. Treadle looms have a number of movable parts controlled by pedals that move the shed up and down. Most of the items made on the treadle loom are cotton or have a cotton warp. The rugs made on them in Madaba and Karak are well-known in Jordan for their softness and near cloth-like appearance and feel. Madaba rugs in particular have become collectors' items because few are made today, and those that are, are not nearly as well-made as they were in the period before 1960.

Art in Clay—Village Pottery

While weaving is the best developed art form among the Bedouin, village women are the creators of much of the traditional pottery in Jordan. Women in the 'Ajlun region in particular were known for their pottery vessels used for a wide variety of purposes. Village women use a range of techniques including the coil or rope method, similar to that developed during the late Neolithic period, and it is hard from simply looking at a broken shard to accurately date a piece of pottery.

Village pottery was, like Bedouin weaving, primarily for use, but women learned various techniques to decorate them. The shaping of any vessel was done by a skilled woman using a smooth piece of wood or a broken piece of old pottery. Once the vessel was finished, it would be left for several days to dry until it had a leathery texture when it would be painted with a light colored slip. If the pottery was to be further decorated, a red paint made from local iron-bearing rock was applied in geometric designs. The vessel would be allowed to dry for several weeks before a final firing would be done, usually in an open fire.

More sophisticated pieces made on a pottery wheel were done by male artisans in urban centers such Hebron or Damascus. During the Ottoman period Damascus became an important center for ceramic production, following the general patterns and methods used in the Turkish ceramic centers such as Iznik. Patterns developed in Iznik, mainly floral designs such as cherry trees in bloom, carnations, and tulips, were adopted in both Damascus and Hebron. Hebron pottery did not achieve the high standards of Damascus, but has endured to the present day. Hebron pottery still uses Ottoman designs but recently has adopted a number of other more local designs inspired from archeological finds including those from Byzantine mosaics and Umayyad frescos from the pleasure palaces and hunting lodges in Jordan.

Art in Straw—Bedouin and Village Basketry

Both Bedouin and village women make plates, trays, and basket containers from straw or palm fronds. Again these pieces are for practical use in daily life, but the women use color to make intricate geometric designs. Among the most beautiful pieces are the large straw trays made to serve food. These are large round trays put on the floor or ground and metal trays with the food are placed on them. Women use straw dyed in bright reds, oranges, yellows, and other colors to make the designs. Some of the more elaborate trays made for special occasions, such as to display a bride's trousseau, may include silk thread in the designs or silk tassels along the edges.

Village women make a number of small boxes from straw and silk thread. These boxes are used to store items such as sewing needles, thread, scissors, and the like. The boxes are suspended by fine chains from the ceilings becoming elements of decoration as well as practical containers. Other containers made of straw or palm fronds include those for bread, fruit, grain, or vegetables. Some of these are lined with leather to protect against humidity.

Art in Silver—Bedouin and Village Silver Jewelry

Silver jewelry was worn by both Bedouin and village women, only the very wealthy elite were able to afford gold jewelry in the past. Traditional jewelry was made by male artisans from the cities or traveling craftsmen who would set up makeshift workshops wherever they happened to be. Work in metals was considered beneath the dignity of Bedouin men, and Bedouin jewelry was made by urban craftsmen for Bedouin customers. Some village jewelry was made by metal workers in the villages, but again most village jewelry was made by urban craftsmen for village clients. Often the same craftsmen made pieces for both Bedouin and villagers. The only traditional pieces made by the women themselves were necklaces that consist of agate and other semiprecious stones, coral, shells, and cloves. Some of these necklaces include ancient beads from even the Neolithic period found in the desert or around old sites. Clove necklaces worn by brides are still part of the wedding traditions among both the Bedouin and villagers.

Traditional silver jewelry for both the Bedouin and village women tend to be large in size and heavy. Bracelets and necklaces tend to be wide and heavy, the amount of silver being a means of insurance for the women in case of divorce or death of her husband. Many of the pieces include designs or amulets to ward off the evil eye from the women and their families, especially children. Charms or *hijab*s with Qur'anic inscriptions for Muslims or images of saints for Christians or with blue beads were commonly made to protect children from harm. Symbols such as the fish, salamander, and frog were used in a number of different forms in much of the silver jewelry.

A variety of techniques were used to make the jewelry: hammering, repoussé, filigree, granulation, sand casting, and niello. The last technique is frequently associated with the Circassians and what is called Circassian or Turkish jewelry. Niello is the use of a black "ink" made of silver, copper, and lead sulfides in a powder form, which is placed in etched or cast designs and then melted. Once hardened the surface is smoothed with a file and the black "ink" causes the design to be better seen. For the niello process to work, and for the niello to stick to the silver, the quality has be fairly high, at least 80 percent silver. Pieces made with lower-quality silver quickly loose the niello. Circassians use niello on their daggers, pistols, handles of riding whips, and saddles. In the past necklaces and bracelets made for Circassian women were often nielloed, and thus the process has been associated with them. One particular type of nielloed bracelet is called *asawir sirkaz* (or Circassian bracelets).

Traditional silver jewelry for Bedouin and village women was made in the past in Karak, al-Salt, and Irbid, in addition to cities in Syria, Palestine, and the Hijaz in Saudi Arabia. One particular type of heavy silver bracelet with a thick central braid was made in Egypt especially for the Bedouin and is called *masriyyah*, meaning Egyptian. Much of the jewelry in Jordan is shared with its neighbors, making it difficult to be able to say if an older piece was made in Jordan or somewhere else. There was, and is yet today, a great deal of exchange in silver jewelry between places as far as Yemen, Central Asia, India, and Egypt. Quality of the silver varies greatly depending on the source, which is usually melted down old pieces or coins. Most of the older silver pieces still found in Jordanian antique shops are higher quality, but since so little of it is still being made (women prefer gold over silver), they are becoming rarer and thus more expensive collectors' items.

Contemporary Arts in Jordan

Since the 1950s Jordan has seen the development of fine arts such as painting and sculpture. Few Jordanian artists have become well-known and the Jordanian public has become more aware of the fine arts since the 1960s. The push for a better appreciation for all of the arts, including theater and music as well as painting and sculpture has been well received in the country. Members of the royal family have given patronage to the arts and to art galleries where it is possible to see the works of Jordanian artists. During the 1970s Jordan's economic elite began buying the art for their homes and by the 1980s there had developed a sophisticated audience. Not only were they interested in modern art, but antiquities became an important part of their tastes as did Jordan's cultural heritage. Pieces of Bedouin or village craft became sought after for their beauty as well as their connection with the cultural identity of the country and its people.

CONCLUSION

Jordanian arts and architecture reflect the more rustic and rural nature of the society. While Jordan is one of the places where man first settled into large urban centers, it has been for much of its history since late antiquity marginalized or a rural hinterland for cities such as Damascus. Weak central government, especially during the Mamluk and Ottoman periods, led to a

Bedouinization of much of the country. The traditional architecture and arts are those of rural villagers and Bedouin for whom utility is an essential part of both architecture and art.

Much of the traditional art are the products of women; tents, rugs, carpets, pottery, and baskets are all objects of daily use but also art. Women are able to express themselves in these objects and the colors and materials they use reflect what is referred to as their mood or their own thoughts. Men also produce both art and architecture in the stone houses found in villages and the more refined crafts such as professional jewelry smiths. Traditional arts and architecture have been able to survive in Jordan despite the pressures of globalization. Jordan's growing middle class values traditional arts, crafts, and architecture, making a local market for sales and an interest in preservation of what is left.

5

Traditional Cuisine and Costume

Jordan's traditional foods and costumes fit within the general region of Greater Syria, which includes Palestine, Lebanon, Syria, and Jordan. The region of Greater Syria as a whole constitutes one of the major divisions of the Arab world and is recognizably different from other cultural regions in the dialects of Arabic spoken, social customs, traditional foods, and traditional costumes. While there are a number of special aspects that make them more recognizably Jordanian than say Syrian or Palestinian, especially in regards to traditional clothing, in general these differences are minor. The region was economically integrated in the past and during the centuries of Islamic rule, major urban centers such as Damascus exercised political, economic, and cultural influence over most of the region. In addition, much of the desert in both Syria and Jordan had been under strong Arab Bedouin influence since antiquity.

TRADITIONAL FOODS OF JORDAN

Jordan's traditional foods fall into several major categories which correspond to the social and cultural makeup of its people. These can be divided into Bedouin, village, Palestinian, and Syrian/Lebanese cuisine, which correspond to the foods of the pastoral nomads, settled villagers, Palestinian refugees, and the village/urban elite with strong Ottoman cultural influence. The national dish of the country is called *mansif* and is the major feast dish of the Bedouin.

Bedouin Foods

As noted above, the national dish of Jordan is the Bedouin *mansif*, which takes its name from the Arabic word meaning "half," as the dish implies that each platter contains half a sheep or goat. *Mansif* is the dish served by Bedouin *shaykh*s at their daily tribal councils or by anyone celebrating an important occasion such as a wedding, a naming ceremony, or to welcome guests. The dish allows the host to demonstrate the wealth, generosity, and hospitality of his family and is always seen as a mark of honor for a guest. It is made of a first layer of a paper-thin type of bread called *shrak* or *marquq* placed on a large serving tray. A huge mound of rice is heaped on the bread and over that is placed lamb or goat meat. Over the whole dish large dippers of a special yogurt sauce made from *jamid,* a rock hard form of yogurt, which is mixed with a small amount of water to make the sauce, are liberally poured over the dish by the host. The meal is eaten with the hands, and pieces of the bread are used to help make balls of rice and meat which are then tossed into the mouth with the flip of the thumb.

There have been adaptations to this dish to accommodate settled or urban life where sheep or goat meat may not be readily found. A smaller version of the traditional *mansif* can be made with chickens, though seen as less noble than using lamb or goat. In addition to the yogurt sauce, the more modern version of the dish may include cooked vegetables such as carrots and potatoes, though some may then argue the dish is no longer a *mansif.*

Mansif is often found in Jordanian restaurants in a much modified version. Instead of the massive meal served up by the Bedouin, the dish is a humble amount of rice on a regular plate while the meat and the sauce are served in a bowl. The wafer-thin bread is also served on the side rather than under the rice. While purists may scoff at this version of the meal, it is nonetheless a popular lunch choice by many Jordanians at local restaurants.

Mansif is the major dish, and it is a meal unto itself, served by the Bedouin and its preparation often includes both the men and the women of a household. The women prepare the bread, rice, and yogurt sauce, but the men prepare the meat. This is especially for when the meal is going to be served as part of a major celebration, such as a wedding feast. Bedouin men state that the most important part of the dish, the meat, must be prepared by them since it is the most "serious" part of it. Women state that while the meat is an essential part, they prepare the "heart" of the dish and without the bread, the rice, and the sauce; the meal would not be a feast. Both parties take the preparation of the dish as serious responsibilities for the success of the meal and of the celebration.

Bedouin, like most pastoral nomads, are not big consumers of meat, but of milk and milk products. Much of their diet is centered around milk from sheep, goats, and, less so today, camels. The type of sheep raised by the Bedouin, the 'Awassi, is a dairy sheep whose milk has always been an important part of the nomads' diet. Though the 'Awassi does not produce the large amounts of milk other eastern Mediterranean breeds do, they are important milk suppliers. Goats are also milked, though their milk is not as sweet as that from 'Awassi ewes. Today fewer Jordanian Bedouin keep herds of camels as they did in the recent past, but female camels are still milked. Milk is either consumed when it is warm and fresh or allowed to sour into something similar to buttermilk, called *rayib*. *Rayib* is the first step towards making the various yogurts that make up much of the Bedouins' diet. Add a small amount of lemon juice and churn it and it becomes butter. Add increasing amounts of salt and it becomes yogurt or sour cream.

Breads are another staple of the Bedouin diet. Flour is one of the major products Bedouin have usually bought from villagers or urban merchants. On occasions when the winter is a good wet one, some Bedouin have grown their own wheat, which they sell or make into flour. Those Bedouin who are only semi-nomadic traditionally have raised a variety of crops including wheat and barley.

Flour is used to make a variety of breads, none of them being made with yeast. Most of the bread consumed by Bedouin is the thin wafer-like *shrak* which is basically flour, salt, and water folded and folded together to make the dough. The dough is spread over a thin convex piece of metal or *saj* that quickly cooks the dough on one side. It is flipped over and the whole process takes only a few minutes for the bread to be ready. *Shark,* also called *marquq* by villagers, is also a common bread for breakfasts in Jordan's villages and even in the cities. It is possible to buy commercially made *shrak* in major supermarkets such as Safeway's, not only in Jordan, but in Saudi Arabia and the Gulf states as well.

A second type of bread common among the Bedouin is one called *khubz min al-tabun*, or literally "bread from an oven," though among the Bedouin no oven as such is used. Instead the bread, which is more of a loaf, is placed in the coals of a fire to bake, but again the dough is basically flour, salt, and water. A bed of hot coals is prepared and the loaf is placed on it. It is then covered with more hot coals and allowed to bake for around five minutes before the coals are removed, the bread dusted off, and served fresh often with home-churned butter.

Important to any Bedouin meal or between meal times are tea and coffee. The preparation of Bedouin coffee, called Arabic coffee to distinguish it from the urban Turkish variety, is a ceremony that calls neighbors to share. The coffee beans are first roasted on an open fire in a special pan that looks like a giant spoon. The beans are constantly turned with a metal stirrer with a long thin handle. The beans are lightly roasted and then poured out into a wooded dish, frequently decorated with brass tacks, and allowed to cool. Once cool, the beans are then poured into a decorated wooden mortar and ground using a special beat that indicates to nearby tents coffee is being prepared. The coffee is poured from the mortar into brass coffee pots, usually made in urban centers such as Damascus or Homs in Syria, and simmered to a boil along with a few pods of cardamom. The cardamom gives the coffee a slight spicy taste, aroma, and a greenish color. The coffee is allowed to come to a boil three times and then is served in tiny ceramic cups with no handle. The amount of coffee is a small, perhaps not even half of the tiny cup, and is served to each person three times. At the end of the third cup it is polite to shake the cup from side to side and say "*da'imeh,*" or "God preserve you." Bedouin consider it polite to offer three cups and for the guest to turn down a fourth. Coffee is always served after a major feast such as *mansif* because it is believed that it helps with digestion.

Tea is also served with a degree of ceremony among the Bedouin, but because it is the everyday, every meal drink, it doesn't have the special social role coffee has. Tea with milk is served first thing in the morning as part of every breakfast. The first glass of tea, always served in small handless glasses, is more milk than tea, and often sweetened canned milk is used. Each succeeding glass has less milk and more tea until the last glasses are only tea. Bedouin make their tea by boiling the sugar and tea leaves in the water, making it both sweet and strong. Every Bedouin tent will have pots of tea either boiling on the fire or staying warm next to the fire all day long ready to serve guests as well as themselves. When a guest has had enough tea, the signal is to turn the glass upside down in front of them or to hand it back to the host with one hand covering the top and say "*da'imeh,*" as one does for politely ending rounds of coffee. Tea is often served before a major feast, or if the family wants to display its hospitality and generosity, three rounds of each, coffee and tea are served. Tea serves as the drink when discussions are in progress while coffee signals the conclusion of deal, sealing an agreement such as a marriage proposal, sale of land, and other major events.

Village Foods

Villagers in Jordan have similar foods to their neighbors in Palestine, Syria, and Lebanon, using a wide variety of vegetables, milk products, poultry, and meats. Absent from much of the Jordanian diet is fish which is culturally not a preferred food. There is strong social prejudice against eating fish though in recent years fewer and fewer people have maintained the prejudice against it. Village foods reflect the ability to produce a larger variety of food stuffs such as olives, citrus fruits, almonds, pistachios, and mulberries in addition to various types of beans, tomatoes, onions, fenugreek, carrots, radishes, beets, and other vegetables. In summer grapes and melons are available. Villagers raise sheep, goats, and cattle as well as chickens, ducks, and geese. All of these contribute their diet.

Village breakfasts are composed of several types of white cheeses made usually from goat or sheep milk; some are salty while others are sweet. Both black and green olives are served along with pickled vegetables such as beets, carrots, and cucumbers. Freshly baked breads served with butter, honey, or fruit preserves are always part of the breakfast. Tea, similar to the Bedouin tea, is served, and in season, fresh juices such as grape, orange, or mulberry are part of the meal.

Lunch is the largest meal and Arab proverbs state that women begin lunch once breakfast has been served. Lunches include at least one meat dish of some kind as the main part of the meal, though Christian families have times when meals are meatless according to their religious calendar. One of the typical dishes is *musakhin* which is made of chicken spiced with sumac and served on Syrian pocket bread (*khubz Suri*). While Palestinians claim *musakhin* as typically Palestinian, it is equally claimed by many Jordanians. The same could be said of nearly all of the traditional Jordanian village dishes.

Lunch is also the time for the wide variety of salads and bread dips made with cracked wheat and fresh vegetables. Salads such as Lebanese *tabbuli* (cracked wheat, parsley, mint, and green onions), *salatah 'arabiyah* (tomatoes, cucumbers, and onions chopped into small pieces with a lemon juice and olive oil dressing), *tahini* dip (sesame paste thinned with lemon juice), eggplant salads and dips such as *Baba Ghanuj* or *m'tabal* (cooked eggplant that has been skinned and then mashed with garlic, lemon juice, and *tahini*) are often part of the meal.

Following the large midday meal, traditionally men would take a rest before going back out to their fields. Women would begin the clean up work from preparing and serving lunch before being able to take a very short rest. Once finished with the rest period, women then begin preparing for their men to return from the fields.

Dinner is not usually as big as lunch, though with the changes in people's work habits it is coming to be more and more like lunch. Traditionally dinner was lighter than lunch and was usually a soup, stew, or other dish that could make use of leftovers from lunch. That which was not eaten was kept for a special end of the week dish using up the old, dry bread, leftover vegetables, and sour cream, called *m'jadrah*. Like many such end of the week dishes, it was a good way to use up what otherwise would be wasted food before there was refrigeration.

Village cuisine includes a variety of spices not always used by the Bedouin. In the spring and fall a number of wild herbs are collected by the women to be dried and used in cooking and in pickling. Spices often found in village dishes include both black and red peppers, sweet pepper, sumac, cinnamon, allspice, cardamom, cloves, and coriander.

Villagers also make tea and coffee similar to that made by the Bedouin. Village tea is often made with mint in the summer and with a sprig of sage in the winter. Sage tea is a traditional means to help prevent colds as well as to help treat a cold or flu. Coffee can be the Bedouin Arabic coffee or the more urban Turkish coffee. Arabic coffee is made with cardamom and no sugar, while Turkish coffee is made with sugar but no cardamom. Villagers are criticized by the Bedouin for not offering their guests the usual three rounds of coffee and tea, but often stop at the second cup, though in the experience of the author plenty of Jordanian and Syrian villagers have offered three cups of each.

Palestinian Foods

Palestinians make up a large portion of Jordan's populations especially in cities such as 'Amman. Palestinians who came to Jordan as refugees starting in 1948 came from a number of social and economic backgrounds, from sophisticated urban elite to pastoral nomads. The loss of lands, shops, and other property had a leveling effect within the refugee community even though many Palestinians subsequently were able to find jobs and fill professional positions. Palestinian foods and traditional clothing (especially for the women) became important ways to help preserve their Palestinian identity.

While much of the traditional foods in Palestine are shared with Jordanians, Syrians, and Lebanese, there are some dishes that are considered more Palestinian than others. One of the typical Palestinian dishes is *maqlubah* (or upside down). *Maqlubah* takes its name from the fact the dish is cooked in reverse order and once finished the pot it is prepared in is placed upside down on a plate and the dish falls out with what had been at the bottom of the pot on top. *Maqlubah* is made with meat (lamb or beef) and onions initially fried in olive oil until lightly brown, a number of vegetables such as cauliflower, potatoes, eggplant, and the like are added along with some water and allowed to simmer. Last, once the vegetables have begun to soften, rice and more water are added. When the rice has turned soft and fluffy the dish is ready to be flipped over onto a serving platter.

Other more Palestinian and Syrian type of foods include *falafel* (or chick pea paste that is deep fried and served with pickles and *tahini* sauce on pocket bread), *kibbeh* (made with cracked wheat and ground meat either made into small balls and stuffed with meat and pine nuts or into a meatloaf), and stuffed vegetables, such as peppers, tomatoes, and potatoes. In addition, several of the more urban types of desserts and sweets were introduced by the

Palestinians. One of the best is *kinafa Nablusi* named for the West Bank city of Nablus. *Kinafa Nablusi* is made of a bottom layer of sweet white cheese covered in shredded phyllo. It is baked until the phyllo begins to brown and then sugar and rosewater syrup is poured over it. Before serving, the top is sprinkled with chopped pistachio nuts.

Ottoman Legacy in Foods

The ruling class for the last 400 years or so of Syria, Lebanon, Palestine, and Jordan were connected to the major centers of Damascus or Cairo. Different foods from the Ottoman Empire were dispersed through official government appointments of peoples from the different ethnicities of the empire. Cities such as Damascus and Aleppo in Syria became well known for their fine cuisine; cuisine that could match that of the capital Istanbul. Jordan is a late comer to the Ottoman legacy in fine cooking as many of the dishes have appeared recently. Jordan was not brought fully into the Ottoman fold until the nineteenth century and had few major urban centers until after World War I. Nonetheless, Jordan has today some of the best restaurants in the region serving fine quality Middle Eastern foods. These include salads, dips, main dishes of meat, poultry, and fish, but even more so in the varieties of sweets and desserts. There is also wider number of spices used beyond those found in village cooking including basil, saffron, cumin, tumeric, and the like. Some of the dishes have names such as The Imam Fainted, each with an interesting story or legend about the origin of the name often related to the imperial kitchens in Istanbul.

One of the new dishes that came with the arrival of Turkish-speaking Uzbeks from Central Asia in the decade after World War I is *riz Bukhari* or Bukharian rice, named for the Central Asian city Bukhara. *Riz Bukhari* is similar to the Arabian Gulf dish called *kabsah* and is made with chicken and lightly browned onions. Once browned, add grated carrots, chopped tomatoes, grated orange or lemon peel, juice of one orange or lemon, spices (cinnamon, allspice, cloves, cardamom, a small amount of black and red pepper, and depending on the person cooking, saffron), and about a cup of water. Then allow the vegetables to begin to cook. The chicken is removed to finish cooking by baking it in an oven while long grain rice is added to vegetables and chicken stock. Once the rice is cooked the dish is served on a platter with the chicken pieces placed on top of the rice and, for the final touch, raisins and chopped almonds are sprinkled over it all.

TRADITIONAL COSTUME

Traditional costume in Jordan is, as noted above, very similar to that found throughout Greater Syria. There are a few differences though, and some of the older designs, especially in women's clothing, are no longer made or used. The breakdown into specific types also follows that of Bedouin, village, and urban. The traditional clothes have been subject to change over time and have never been static. Like all fashion, they are dictated by tastes and availability of cloth as well as the need to be practical and functional. Of the ethnic minorities in Jordan, only the Circassians and Shishans have preserved their own traditional clothing, which they wear for special occasions.

Bedouin Costume

Bedouin costume has undergone a number of changes since the nineteenth century when European travelers took photos and wrote extensive narratives describing it . The largest and most significant changes have occurred in women's costume while men's, though changed, has not been altered as much.

Men's Costume

Men's costume is simple, consisting of cotton trousers called *sirwal* over which a long, ankle-length shirt called *dishdashah* is worn. *Dishdashah*s can be made of different kinds and weights of cloth with lighter cottons and synthetics usually worn in the summers and heavier cottons, linens, and now synthetic blends worn in the winter. Since the 1970s cheap synthetic cloth from Asia has replaced the better-quality cottons and wools that had been imported from Britain and India. Unlike in some of the nearby countries, Jordanian Bedouin do not wear light colors or white in summer and reserve dark colors for the winter, but are open to any color any time of year; however, different shades of blue tend to be the most common color choices.

The *dishdashah* is usually belted with a wide leather belt or with one that combines leather and a form of plaiting of which the best is still made in Damascus. The belt may also be one that straps over the shoulders with places for bullets and a holster for a pistol. Men usually have a large, sharp dagger called *shabriyyah* strapped to their belts. The dagger is used as an all-purpose tool for repairs to equipment such as saddles, tents, and even motor vehicles. In addition to the leather belt, some men may wear a long round braided cord made of silk that ends in two large tassels. The cord is wrapped around both the waist and over the shoulders and is tied on the right side, allowing the tassels to hang down nearly to the knee.

Over the *dishdashah* men may wear an outer cloak called *bisht* or *'abbayah* which can be made of a number of different types of cloth from homespun wool to fine camel hair or even silk. The better quality ones are made of camel hair and have gold or silver thread embroidery down the front and along the seams down the arms and around the openings for the hands. Those of lesser quality have similar embroidery in cotton or cotton silk (cotton thread stretched until it has the same sheen as silk). In recent decades synthetic cloth from Asia has replaced real silk and to a degree camel hair; these are substantially cheaper and easier to afford for the average person.

In the winter Bedouin men wear a large, heavy coat made of lamb's fleece called *farw*, which means a pelt. The lamb pelts are cut and sewn together with the fleece side showing to make the inner lining of the coat, which is made of heavy cotton, wool, or camel hair. The finer ones are heavily decorated with appliqué or cotton embroidery in special workshops mainly in Damascus and can cost up to $800. The less expensive variety is made of two heavy wool blankets cut and sewn to make a coat. Again, the coat is decorated with appliqué. Since the early 1980s a cheap form to the coat has become available replacing real lamb skins with synthetic fleece. While they have the look of the finer quality coats the cost is closer to $40.

The man's head cloth has a range of names but is usually called *shimagh* or *kuffiyah* in Jordan. It is a large, square, often red or black checkered cloth of cotton or cotton and silk blend. The higher amount of silk, the finer the piece, and the more expensive it is. The cloth is folded into a triangle, the better quality being better able to be an even triangle, and placed on the head so that the peak of the triangle falls down the wearer's back. In Jordan the *shimagh* is often trimmed in tiny tassels and each of the four ends of the cloth have long, elaborate tassels added to them. The use of tassels is a distinctive feature of Jordanian *shimagh* and sets Jordanians off from their neighbors. Many Bedouin wear it throwing the two-side ends up over the back of the head. The two ends are tightened making almost a bun with it.

The *shimagh* is held in place on the head by means of a double coiled head rope made of tightly braided and wrapped goat hair called *'aqal*. The head rope also comes in a wide range of styles and sizes from fairly cheap, loosely made ones to extremely fine ones that end in a series of long tassels that hang down to the midback of the wearer. Many Jordanians prefer to wear the ones with a number of long back tassels while those of Palestinian origin prefer those with one single back cord that ends in a short crosspiece. Those who prefer to identify more with Syria and Syrian tribes wear the ones that fit on the crown of the head, are very thin, and end in a long cord with a design such as moon and crescent. Those with closer ties to tribes in Saudi Arabia wear the Saudi style head rope, which has with no extra back decorations and is worn more to the front of the head. The way the *'aqal* is worn tells a good deal about the person, not only the country he may wish to be identified with, but also whether he is single and wears it at a jaunty angle to the side or is married and wears it straight on the head.

Women's Costume

Women's costumes have had the greatest change over the past hundred years. There have been important changes in styles of dresses, head scarves, and even jewelry worn. Bedouin women's clothes have been influenced by those worn by village and urban women they have been in contact with, availability of types of cloth or embroidery thread in the market, and other forces of fashion and economy.

The main part of a Bedouin woman's wardrobe is a long, ankle length black dress. In the nineteenth century and into the first part of the twentieth century, these were the huge *thob 'ob* or *khalagah* (or double dress). The dress was made to be nearly twice the length of the woman and the extra cloth was pulled up and over a wide belt to form a doubled dress. The sleeves were also extralong and extrawide and tied behind the back to be out of the way from work while one was also pulled over the head and tied in place with a wide cloth headband. Sleeves were made to be wide and long so they could have multiple uses, such as keeping keys and other items that need to be handy, and even holding babies.

The dresses were decorated with embroidery along the neck and down the front, along the side seams and the bottom hem, and along the sleeves. The embroidery helped reinforce the dress and strengthen it against the heavy use women made of them. As a result, the embroidery wasn't always in even patterns or symmetrical designs but often was asymmetrical and looked a bit off when the dress was not being worn. When being worn, with one sleeve tied over the head and tied behind the woman's back, as well as with the extra cloth looped over a belt, the designs are less off and take on more symmetrical patterns.

Some Bedouin women's dresses have been influenced by those of village women for some time. In the northern part of Jordan in particular, both village and Bedouin women have embroidered their dresses with patterns where the exposed cloth makes the pattern. The embroidery is done in horizontal strips of nearly even width, each made with a different color of silk or cotton floss. This type of embroidery is a distinctive feature of villages in northern Jordan and some of the Bedouin tribes who used to migrate between northern Jordan and northern Palestine. The work needed to make even one strip takes a good deal of time—the patterns being made by the exposed dress material—and few women make them today.

Many Jordanian Bedouin women have been influenced by the dresses made and worn by Palestinian women and the Bedouin from southern Palestine (the Negev) and Sinai. The dresses made and worn by the Negev and Sinai Bedouin are heavily worked silk or cotton embroidery in bright colors such as yellow, red, and orange. Among the women from tribes in the Negev and Sinai, dresses with a large amount of blue are worn by young, unmarried women while married women use designs in bright colors. Women who are widowed often switch back to blue embroidery but keep a small amount of color in the chest panel and around the neck. The designs tend to be more geometric and floral than many of the designs used by settled village women in Palestine. Again the sleeves are large and wide allowing them to have multiple uses by the wearer and tied behind the back to keep them out of the way of work.

In more recent years a smaller, modified version of the older large Bedouin dress has become fashionable. The sleeves are no longer the huge, wide ones but are fairly small. They are still tied behind the back, leaving the women's arms full mobility to work. The front of the dress has a small chest panel embroidered in bright colors, such as yellow or red, in floral patterns. Sometimes dresses for special occasions may also have floral patterns on the lower part of the skirt, especially on the back panel. Women wear a long sleeved shirt underneath the dress so that their arms are not exposed.

Bedouin women usually belt their dresses using a wide leather, woven wool, or cloth belt. The belt's color also can tell a good deal about the woman in that the color red is reserved for married women. The woven wool belts are made by the women themselves and are often made of natural colored wool with small bands of black goat hair and decorated with buttons and cowrie shells. This type of belt is rarely found in Jordan and is associated much more with tribes in the Negev and Sinai. Leather belts are made in Damascus or other cities in Syria, but more commonly, women simply use a long piece of colored cloth as a belt. Red is usually reserved for married women and unmarried women wrap a blue or dark colored cloth around their waist.

The head is covered with a thin, black crepe-like cloth called a *shambar* or *milfa'* which is wrapped under the chin and over the head so that if she needs to, the wearer can bring it over her mouth and nose as a veil. The head cloth is held in place by another long piece of cloth folded lengthwise to form a wide band and tied around the head called *'asabah.* Some of the women prefer to use a silk or silk and cotton brocade cloth made in Homs for the headband. Other women tie the headband in such a way as to form a peak, in some instances the women shape the headbands into extremely tall peaks or cones. This fashion is found more among younger women than older ones and is more prevalent among those Bedouin with strong ties to tribes in Syria.

In the past, teenage girls wore various types of caps with long tails running down the back often heavily embroidered and decorated in charms, coins, buttons, beads, and cowrie shells. In some instances the tail was so long as to drag behind the girl when she walked, supposedly to "wipe away her footprints." A form of this decorated cap is still worn at special occasions in Jordan and Syria by Bedouin women. This is the 'arjah, which has a main structure of metal links that go around the head and another piece that goes over the head from front to back. The head band is made of colorful bead-work and the tail is made of fine brocade or some other colored cloth and decorated with coins and charms. The tail ends in a number of large silk tassels, which keep it hanging straight.

Village Costume

Traditional village costume differs a little from that of the Bedouin though, in the past, villagers visited major cities and were able to purchase more expensive materials. They had close economic connection with urban people, including urban elite, and, if able to afford it, tried to emulate urban fashions. Introductions included the Turkish *tarbush* (the tall red hat with a long black silk tassel), western-cut men's jacket, as well as other urban fashion changes.

Men's Costume

Traditional dress for village men is very similar to that of the Bedouin. Men wore a cotton shirt buttoned down the front, a cotton vest embroidered along the front and the neck, and around the sleeves and bottom, a wide leather or cloth belt, and the loose fitting Turkish trousers made of cotton. The trousers worn by Bedouin men frequently had straight legs and were not as baggy as that worn by village men, who traditionally preferred the type that were very baggy and had narrow cuffs that came down only to the calf of the leg. Village men wore the same kind of long, ankle-length shirt *dish-dashah* over the other shirt and vest or, similar to the villagers in Palestine, an overcoat called *qumbaz* that buttoned or tied at the left shoulder and on the left at the waist. The coat was belted with a narrow leather belt and the two bottom ends could be tucked up into the belt to allow better leg movement during work. The *qumbaz* was made of good-quality cotton or cotton and wool blends imported from Britain or of silk or cotton silk blends made in Syria. Today few men wear either the *dishdashah* or *qumbaz* though they may lounge in them in the house. Generally only older men still wear them and younger men now wear western jeans and shirts.

Village men still wear the *shimagh* and 'aqal as do the Bedouin. Villagers wear the same range of style, colors, and favor those with the distinctive Jordanian tassels. Only the plain white *shimagh* may not have tassels added to it. No one wears the Turkish *tarbush,* though in the later part of the nineteenth century and the early part of the twentieth century some village men wore it with an embroidered cloth made in Syria wrapped around it. The *shimagh* is practical headgear and it is not unusual to see Jordanian men wearing it along with otherwise western clothes.

Women's Costume

Traditional costumes worn by village women demonstrate a number of influences and their access to products made in major urban centers such as Damascus, Homs, and Aleppo. A number of Jordanian villages have historical connections to villages in Palestine or southern Syria and their embroidery reflects these ties. In southern Jordan, the ties have been to local Bedouin tribes as well as those in the Negev, Sinai, and the northern Hijaz. More elite women adopted styles from the urban elite, though often in a more conservative form. Since the 1940s change in village clothes has been rapid and it is not unusual to see several generations in the same family wearing widely different fashions.

The main feature of village women's costume, like that of the Bedouin women, is the dress. During the nineteenth century and into the early twentieth century some village women also wore the huge *khalagah* or double dress, however, many wore a long, ankle length dress, usually of black cotton or cotton and wool blend, which was richly embroidered with colorful silk or cotton floss. Jordanian women did not cover them with the massive amounts of fine embroidery, as is the practice of many Palestinian women, though they did use many of the same types of floral and geometric patterns favored by the Bedouin yet today. Some women embroidered their dresses along the seams with alternating red, white, and yellow floss, and the chest panels were merely marked out and an X embroidered through the middle. Instead of embroidering patterns on the dresses, some village women used purchased rickrack and then sewed it on as appliqué. In northern Jordan many of the women used to make the embroidered dresses where the exposed cloth made the pattern. As with the Bedouin dress of the same style, the embroidery was done as different colored strips on the skirt of the dress and around the sleeves. In southern Jordan, women from the town of Ma'an wore huge dresses of alternating green and red silk panels. They were not heavily embroidered but otherwise looked very similar to the Palestinian *malikah* or royal dress common in the Jerusalem-Bethlehem region. Unlike Bedouin women who usually belted their dresses and where belts were indicators of social status, village women did not always use belts. In addition, village dresses rarely had the long-wide sleeves common among the Bedouin, but often the sleeves were tight fitting down to the wrist. Today very few village women wear traditional costume except at special occasions like weddings and many no longer embroider.

Village women often wore heavily embroidered jackets over their dresses when going out. These were not usually home made, but purchased in cities such as Jerusalem or Damascus. Those that were made at home looked like small versions of the men's *farw* coats, but without the inner lining of lamb's fleece.

Village women also wore similar head covers to the Bedouin; a crepe like scarf wrapped about the head also called *shambar* and held in place with another cloth tied around the head also called *'asabah*. Some village women added a bit of red embroidery or dyed the bottom parts of the *shambar* red following fashions in Syria. Village women favored the heavy silk brocade cloth made in Homs for the *'asabah* or used a men's *shimagh* folded and tied as a headband. Again, like the Bedouin, young girls wore embroidered caps decorated with charms, silver coins, shells, buttons, and beads. The caps also had long tails running down the girl's back though rarely as long as some of the worn by Bedouin girls. Today these have been replaced with a head scarf if the girl wears any head cover at all.

Palestinian Costume

As a result of the conflicts between the Arabs and the Israelis, many Palestinians have sought refuge in nearby states including Jordan. For several decades the West Bank was incorporated into Jordan and the flow of people and goods was open. Jordanian cities such as 'Amman have large Palestinian populations, as much as 50 percent of the total. While Palestinians are similar in many ways to Jordanians and there have been long historical ties between the two peoples, there are some differences in costume. Maintaining specifics of costume among the Palestinians has been an important means of preserving their own identity.

Men's Costume

Palestinian men's traditional costume needs to be divided between that of the urban areas such as Jerusalem or Hebron, villagers, and Bedouin. Urban men were more subject to the changes in fashions in other major urban centers such as Cairo, Beirut, Damascus, and Istanbul. By the end of the nineteenth century the modified European dress adopted in Cairo, Damascus, and Istanbul had already replaced other more traditional clothes. Only villagers and Bedouin retained less western costumes.

During the first three decades of the twentieth century costume worn by village and Bedouin men became more and more alike. Village men adopted the Bedouin *kuffiyah* and *'aqal* replacing a small turban made of embroidered cloth from Syria. The adoption of similar headgear was a result of the

Palestinian resistance movement and the need to blend the local populations against British attempts to identify rebels. The change was first implemented by young village and even urban men and generally adopted during the Palestinian uprising in the 1930s. As a result there was a generalization of dress; the *qumbaz* and *kuffiyah* with *'aqal*. This has remained Palestinian men's dress to the present day.

Women's Costume

Palestinian women have retained the specifics of regionalism or even home village to the present day. From a woman's dress, the practiced eye can easily tell the district or village a woman is from, and even if she is Muslim or Christian. Palestinian women developed the art of embroidery and certain designs, colors, and even type of floss (gold thread for example), which was adopted in the course of the sixteenth to twentieth centuries. There was a flowering of embroidery in the late nineteenth and early twentieth centuries when cheaper silk floss from France was introduced. In addition, a number of European embroidery pattern books became available, enlarging the corpus of designs beyond the older floral and geometric designs. Palestinian women used a wide variety of cloth for their dresses as well: red, green, and blue cloth woven in the Palestinian cities of Majdal, Safad, and Bethlehem; silks from Damascus and Homs; and imported cloths from Europe. Instead of the usual black worn by Jordanian women, Palestinian women's dresses are in a number of colors such as white, green, red, as well as the multicolored royal dress.

Palestinian women traditionally wore embroidered or silk caps decorated with silver or gold coins. Some local styles included a heavy silver chin strap that hung underneath the chin and ended in a heavy silver pendant. In the region of Bethlehem women wore a high cap decorated with silver or gold coins and coral. Over the cap women wore a long embroidered head cloth called a *khirqah*. The cloth was often cotton or linen strips sewn together and richly embroidered with similar designs as on her dress. While in recent years many Palestinian women wear the caps only for special holidays or events, but they have retained the *khirqah* for daily use.

Circassian Costume

The Circassians and Shishans are relatively new arrivals to Jordan but have greatly assimilated into the Arab population today. They have preserved their national dress for special occasions. The men wear a costume very similar to that of the Russian Cossack with a tall fur hat usually made of lambskin, a frock coat that reaches to the knees, long, straight legged trousers, and high leather riding boots. The coat is belted with a leather belt which attaches to the back crisscrossing the chest and over the shoulders. In the belt, men wear a pistol and a dagger, both of these highly decorated with silver mountings.

Women wear several layers of long dresses over which they wear a colorful coat made of brocade or print cloth. They wear a rather tall embroidered cap over which they drape a long piece of cloth, which falls down the woman's back.

CONCLUSION

Jordan is part of the cultural area of Greater Syria. Though it shares a good deal with its neighbors of Palestine, Lebanon, and Syria, it nonetheless has its own distinctive features in dialect, food, and dress. These distinctly Jordanian features relate to the history of the country and the strong rural, Bedouin and village, origin of the Jordanian identity. Palestinians living in Jordan have preserved their own distinctive features and, though of the same religions and culture as their Jordanian neighbors, have maintained their own identity, especially through women's clothes and foods. As in many parts of the Arab world, dress and foods are important aspects of a person's individual and group identity.

The Yarmuk River separates Jordan (in the foreground) from Syria (in the background). The Battle of the Yarmuk was fought near here. Courtesy of the author.

Abu Shahir is a proud member of the Bidul tribe, who have lived in area of Petra for generations. Courtesy of the author.

General view of the city of al-Salt, one of Jordan's main cities that dates back into antiquity. Courtesy of the author.

Downtown 'Amman in the old heart of the city. The two minarets of the Hussein Mosque are visible in the background. Courtesy of the author.

The Neolithic site al-Baydah in southern Jordan is one of the oldest settlement (village) sites in the world. Courtesy of the author.

Harvest season (early June) in the northern Jordanian village of Hartha. Courtesy of the author.

A Bedouin tent of the Bidul tribe at al-Baydah, north of Petra, makes use of a Nabatean ruin for a smooth, flat floor surface and a sacrificial block for a table. Courtesy of the author.

Roman period ruins of Umm al-Jamal in northern Jordan. This was a Nabatean trading city. Today camels belonging to Sardiyah Bedouin graze among the ruins. Courtesy of the author.

Typical "throne" house in the northern village of Umm Qays. Courtesy of the author.

al-Salt has a large number of late Ottoman buildings. Courtesy of the author.

Late Ottoman period homes in the heart of al-Salt. al-Salt has some of the best preserved late Ottoman period buildings in Jordan. Courtesy of the author.

Qasr Bint al-Far'un, or the Palace of the Pharaoh's Daughter, is one of the very few freestanding buildings in ancient Petra that has withstood the massive earthquakes that tumbled most of the site. Courtesy of the author.

The Ashrafiyyah Mosque in 'Amman uses alternating layers of black basalt and white limestone. This building style is more common in northern Jordan, where both stones are found. Courtesy of the author.

King 'Abdallah Mosque blends older architectural styles with modern concepts. The mosque, built in the early 1980s, has become one of the most recognizable buildings in the country. Courtesy of the author.

Gedara, now called Umm Qays, is one of the Decapolis cities. The white marble statue locally called "Umm Qays" or "Mother of Qays" was in the center of the amphitheater. Courtesy of the author.

Father and son enjoy a typical Jordanian breakfast. Courtesy of the author.

Bedouin woman of the Bidul tribe in southern Jordan baking *khubz min al-tabun* in the coals of the fire. Courtesy of the author.

Bedouin man of the Sa'idiyyin tribe of southern Jordan roasts coffee beans for Arabic coffee. Courtesy of the author.

Young Bedouin of the Sa'idiyyin tribe in southern Jordan serving Arabic coffee to guests. Courtesy of the author.

Bedouin men of the Bidul tribe cook the meat for a *mansif* or Bedouin feast of lamb. Courtesy of the author.

A wedding feast in the northern Jordanian village of Kharjah. The groom's brothers help serve the guests sitting under a Bedouin tent. Courtesy of the author.

Bedouin newlyweds of the 'Ammarin tribe of southern Jordan standing in front of their wedding tent, where the bride receives visitors. Courtesy of the author.

Young Bedouin girl of the Bidul tribe of southern Jordan spinning goat hair into yarn. Other members of the family look on. Courtesy of the author.

Settled Bedouin of 'Ajarmah tribe with one of his Arabian horses. Desert bred Arabian horses are still important to many Bedouin in Jordan. Courtesy of the author.

6

Gender, Marriage, and Family

Jordanian society is conservative whether referring to the Muslim majority or the Christian minority. The conservative nature of the society and the very strong family bonds are reflected in what is considered as appropriate dress, behavior, and gender relations. In recent decades there have been some changes in the overall attitude of the country about such things as dating, but Jordan remains a strongly conservative society.

FAMILY AND FAMILY STRUCTURE

Family is the basis for Jordanian society and is one of its major strengths. Like most Arab family structures, the Jordanian family is patriarchal with the male head of household as the major decision maker and the main disciplinarian. Traditionally, the senior male was the head of a large, extended household where it was common until into the 1970s for several generations to live in either the same house or in closely clustered housing. While in public the head of the household made the decisions, which were given order-like to all of the other members of the group, in private women had an important say in all matters that concerned the family. Private discussions held in the bedroom where even other family members could not hear were where the real decisions were made. The head of the household discussed matters with his wife and mother, if she lived with them, and together they made the decisions, though in public women's voices were not heard.

The head of the household held the supreme position within the family structure and his wife, mother, eldest sister, or whoever was the most senior of the women held a nearly equal position. The other members of the family, adult sons and their wives and children, unmarried sons and daughters all held well-understood positions within the family hierarchy. Males held socially superior status, even over elder sisters, and a much younger brother could forbid his elder sister from leaving the house or require that he as the male accompany her. Those women who married into the family kept their social position within their father's and later brother's households and gained position within their husbands' families only after becoming mothers of sons. Until she became the mother of a son, her position was the lowest in the family hierarchy with the least voice.

It was important to both men and women to have sons. Social standing for both was connected to being able to be called "Father of" (*Abu*) or "Mother of" (*Umm*) the first male child, resulting in names such as Abu Muhammad or Umm Khalid. Some names were linked to Islamic or Christian traditions such as if the father's name was Ibrahim, the child was often called Khalil thus, even before marriage a man might be called Abu Khalil based on long traditions of naming children. Once a person became "Father of" or "Mother of", people preferred to refer to them this way rather than use their given names.

In the traditional family, the closest relations were often cross gendered. That is, the strongest relationships were between fathers and their daughters, mothers and their sons, and brothers and sisters. These bonds reflected the needs of the traditional, extended family system, and where there were no other social networks to take care of divorced, widowed, or aged family members. The strong bonds between fathers and brothers with their daughters and sisters stemmed from the fact that, although she moved into another household when married, she did not join her husband's family. She remained a member of her own family, did not change her family name to that of her husband, and could always count on the protection of her father and brothers should she need it. If a woman was abused or unhappy in her husband's house, she could seek the protection of her father or brothers who were duty bound by social custom to take her side. Mothers needed similar protection of their sons once they had grown old with no other male to provide for them.

The head of the household gave orders to all of the other members of the family and expected to be obeyed out of respect as well as out of duty and responsibility. It was considered to be the mark of a bad family should sons, daughter, daughters-in-law, or any member of the household argue back or refuse to do as they were told. When the patriarch gave an order that seemed contrary to the general will of family members, they would appeal not to him, but to the most senior of the women to intercede with him on their behalf. If asked in private particularly by his wife or mother to change his mind, it would be difficult to refuse, and while not challenged in public, he would usually listen to them. The women could employ a wide range of subtle pressures, such as late meals, badly cooked foods, or sloppy housework, should he refuse to listen to their appeals. The house would return to normal once he changed his mind.

In the traditional family the men were responsible for the public sphere including income generation. Boys began accompanying their fathers once they were no longer considered to be children and needed to be in the company of men rather than women. This began around the age of eight and boys would be required to spend an increasing amount of time away from the protection of their mothers. In the traditional family the public role of the male was learned at an early age. Many of the travelers in the nineteenth and first part of the twentieth centuries were astonished at the ability of young boys to act as hosts during visits to families. Taking their responsibility as males seriously, these young boys would take the place of older male relatives when they were absent and act as host for visitors. Not only would they take the role of welcoming the guest, but they would prepare tea and coffee and slaughter a sheep or goat for the guest's meal.

Women were expected to remain at home, but were often called upon to help with planting, harvesting, and winnowing crops, or herding, especially small stock such as sheep and goats. While women often assisted in farm labor or herding livestock, their primary duty was to maintain well-ordered households. Women managed the house and were responsible for shopping, cooking, cleaning, spinning, weaving, making clothes, and child rearing. Young girls began to assist their mothers at an early age and often girls as young as five or six years old would be given tasks such as to fetch water from a fountain or spring, or to watch and care for younger siblings. By the time she was twelve, a girl was able to do nearly all the tasks required to be a good wife and mother.

One of the most important concepts to maintain the good reputation of a family was and to a great extent is yet today honor (the opposite of which is shame). Honor is linked to the behavior of the members of a family, especially for the women. An Arab proverb says that the honor of a family rides on the skirts of its women, meaning that women carry the greatest share of a family's reputation. In a traditional family women are to be modest in dress, manners, and speech. Boys are more indulged and some bad behavior can be excused as youthful energy, but still such indulgence has its limits. Boys who gain reputations for poor manners, rude speech, and lack of proper respect are considered a family shame. In a society like Jordan's, where there is a strong traditional value of group rather than individual, the bad reputation of one family member has direct impact on the group as a whole. A family with a bad member is itself judged as a bad family and others would be reluctant to marry into it for fear of being also considered bad. It is important to maintain a good reputation that respects the concept of honor.

Despite important changes in recent decades, the family remains an important part of Jordanian culture. Respect for elders is still found, though few still kiss their fathers' or mothers' hands whenever they enter their presence as they did before as a public recognition of this respect. Honor and the reputation of being a good family are still important values to Jordanians. The family structure has had to adapt to rapid economic, political, and social changes and, though many families today are no longer the traditional extended type, the cultural values it represented are still respected.

Gender

Gender relations are guided by the principles of a deeply Muslim people. Though some 15 to 20 percent of Jordanians are Christians, they share many of the same conservative values as are articulated by their Muslim neighbors. Jordan was a largely rural society until the 1950s and the traditional, conservative values held by Jordanians reflect this heritage. Men and women in rural communities, whether Bedouin or villager, were able to meet and talk, strict social rules maintained a degree of social distance between them.

In Bedouin society women have always had greater freedom of movement than among settled peoples in the Middle East. The very nature of pastoral nomadism requires women to take active roles in the daily activities of the family. Women need to leave the protection of the tent to find fuel and fetch water on a daily basis. Young unmarried girls are often required to tend flocks of sheep and goats while the males deal with larger and more difficult livestock such as camels. Men have frequently had to be gone for extended times, either herding camels or working in towns and cities, leaving women and children to take care of matters at home. Bedouin women have long done their own marketing, selling rugs and other woven items, milk, milk products, or even their own livestock, as well as buying supplies from village and urban merchants. Bedouin women's involvement in the family's income activities has meant that they are able to have a greater say in family matters.

Bedouin women make the decision to stay on the male side of the tent when guests arrive or not. While male guests are required to stay on the male, public side of the tent, the women of the tent have the option to move from the public to the private side. Even if they have decided to move to the private, female side of the tent, women may join the conversation through the curtain that divides the sections.

Village women have also been required by the necessity of work to leave the house and engage in marketing activities with men. Women frequently had to assist the men of the household in agricultural labor, but with the men of their household present. Strong social conventions about family honor and reputation limit the types of interactions as well as the proper place and time for them to meet. Women could go to the market on their own, but only in the weekly markets or in urban markets where she was under the watchful eye of family and family friends. Girls under 15 years of age and women over 50 years of age had greater freedom of movement and greater ability to interact with strangers in places like markets. Village and urban women in Jordan traditionally have had less freedom of movement than that of Bedouin women, but more so than many village and urban women in many other parts of the Islamic world. While Jordanians are conservative, they are also practical. Attempts to restrict and segregate attendance at school sports events by Islamic fundamentalists in the 1990s resulted in them losing seats in parliament in the following elections.

Jordanian women have held high positions in the government since the 1960s though these were appointed positions by the King or various ministers. Jordanian women did not run for elected offices until the 1980s and were not elected until the election of 1993 when Tujan al-Faisal became the first woman elected to parliament. Women have entered the job market in increasing numbers as well. The Royal Family has promoted the greater public participation of women and many of the Royal women are well-known figures both inside and outside of Jordan. Jordan's queens have been involved in social development and the promotion of women since the early 1970s as have a number of the princesses. Several have established important high profile social service foundations. Jordan has one of the highest literacy rates in the Arab world for both men and women. Jordanian women have sought university degrees since the founding of the University of Jordan, while women from the elite Palestinian families have been seeking higher degrees since the 1920s. Jordanian women are far from the meek, secluded picture many have of the traditional, conservative Muslim woman. Jordanian women are found in nearly every field of work. For example, Jordan is the first Arab country to have women taxi drivers (who take only women passengers). Soon after Jordan's first woman taxi driver was made known to the broader Arab world through newspaper articles, Egypt also began having women taxi drivers.

Jordanians have found interesting ways to maintain important cultural values but adapt them to the changing times. For example, Jordan is the first Arab country to have women-only coffeehouses. In the past, the coffee house was a male space where no women would be found, at least no respectable woman. In 2004 the first coffeehouse for women opened in 'Amman where women can go after work, relax with friends over cups of coffee or tea, smoke a water pipe, listen to music, and talk just as the men have done for centuries. The only men allowed are those who work in the kitchen. Husbands, fathers, and brothers have taken to the idea since the place is respectable, owned and managed by women, and no men are allowed. Important cultural values of honor are not compromised by the women only coffeehouse, but are upheld in a new more contemporary way.

MARRIAGE CUSTOMS

Marriage customs in Jordan have changed greatly in the past several decades from the traditional style taking several days to a week to celebrate to a more western influenced one-day event. Today most Jordanian weddings are hardly distinguishable from those of any of the nearby countries, Palestine, Lebanon, Syria, and Egypt. The traditional wedding was a large affair that took place at the homes of both the groom and the bride. Similar to many other aspects of culture in Jordan, the main differences in customs were between Bedouin and villagers, with the villagers having many customs in common with villagers in Palestine and Syria.

Most Bedouin still try to maintain traditional wedding celebrations that last between five to seven days. The preferred marriage is between first cousins, what is called *ibn 'Amm* or the father's brother's son. In the past the *ibn 'Amm* had the right of first say before a girl could be married and only if he gave up his right could she accept the marriage proposal from another man. The main purpose behind such close marriages was, and is, to keep the family's property within the family since girls inherited their own share from their fathers. In Bedouin society women frequently control their own property and inheritance without the interference of their husbands. Thus to keep major economic assets from leaving the family, marriages were encouraged between fairly close family members.

When a young man wanted to get married, he and his father would discuss the matter with the women of the family who would have a better idea of which girls, including his cousins, would make suitable wives. Often the young man would have begun a quiet courtship talking to the girl as she went about her daily tasks and volunteering to act as the guard when the girls take the sheep and goats out to graze. In a close-living society such as the Bedouin, there are a number of opportunities for young people to meet and talk without compromising the girl's honor, especially if they are relatives. Once the young man's parents agree he can be married, he and his father visit the tent of the intended bride. They come formally dressed to indicate the seriousness of the visit. The father of the bride, seeing their formal dress, will dress himself up in similar clothes and then come to greet them on the men's side of the tent. The discussion will begin and should both parties agree to the wedding, it is sealed with coffee.

Depending on the amount of materials that need to be prepared, the wedding may take place shortly afterwards. The bride is expected to bring with her much of the tent's furnishings called the *jihaz* and it is a chance for her and the women of her family to display their talents in weaving. She may, for example, have a tent she has made ready for their new home. The bride and her female relatives make and embroider her wedding clothes and those she will take with her. The groom's family sends out invitations (usually this is done orally with the young men of the family dispatched to carry the message) to all of the nearby tents, whether from their tribe or not and the larger the number invited the better for the family's reputation. Invitations will be sent to the tribal leadership as well and usually the *shaykh*s attend. The groom's family begins gathering all of the food they will need to provide a feast for the guests.

The week of the wedding celebration begins with small evening gatherings at the tents of both the bride and groom. These begin as small affairs and as each night progresses to the final wedding day, they increase in size numbers invited, and amount of food served, especially at the groom's tent. At the groom's tent the men present dance and sing or shoot joy shots into the air with their rifles or pistols. At the bride's tent the gathering is more of a women's affair and culminates in the *henna* night when the bride's hands and feet are decorated with a paste made from the *henna* plant which stains the skin a red color. The paste is applied to the skin and then wrapped in cloth to allow it to dry and set the designs. The length of time the paste is left on the skin relates to how deep the color is and how long it will be visible; the longer it is left on, the deeper the color and longer it will last.

The day of the wedding the groom is made ready by his male relatives and close friends who shave him after he has bathed. He dresses in new clothes and waits for the arrival of his bride a bit later in the day. As he waits the guests begin to arrive and congratulate him. The women of his family begin to make the wedding feast of *mansif* (see the chapter on foods), cleaning and cooking the rice as well as preparing the yogurt sauce. The men of his family slaughter the sheep, goats, or camels—it is believed the meat needs to be consumed soon after an animal is slaughtered—and cut them into pieces to be cooked in large pots over open fires. Other members of the family and the groom's friends keep rounds of coffee and tea going as guests continue to arrive.

The bride, once dressed in her wedding dress, puts on jewelry which usually includes a necklace made of cloves and a number of silver (and now more often gold) bracelets, and a large silk cloth (often green in color) covering her whole head; she is brought from her tent by her female relatives and seated on a horse that is led by her closest male kinsmen. Other men of her family, cousins and uncles, ride in front of her making daring dashes and shooting off their guns. The procession is followed by the women and young people of her family who sing and clap or carry various parts of her *jihaz,* or all of the things she would need for her own household including furniture.

When she arrives at the groom's tent, she is quickly taken to a small, separate tent set up just for the young couple. The groom is then brought to the tent to consummate the marriage. Once this has been done, the bride is visited by the women who come to congratulate her while the groom rejoins the guests. The feast is served once it is finished cooking, and men and women eat separately. When the meal has been eaten, last rounds of coffee are served and the guests begin to depart.

The bride remains in the separate tent for seven days visited only by the groom and women. This time marks her transition from a single woman in her father's tent to a married woman in her husband's tent. Among Bedouin who are now settled, a room within the house serves the same purpose. When the seven days is over, the women of the groom's family take her out to a well or water source where the bride is washed and dressed in her first regular clothes as a married woman. She then is ready to take her place in her husband's household.

Traditional village weddings are a long process that begins with the engagement. In the past the young couple was not usually actively involved in selection of their partner, but the elder women of the two families would feel out the prospects. This would be done where women could meet and discuss their children with each other such as at the market or at the public bathhouse. Christian women used the occasion of mass on Sunday. These were places where the women could observe the young girls and judge their honor. Should the elder women decide that the available son and daughter were of good families and would make a good husband or wife, the women would then tell the matter to the men of the two households. The father of the groom accompanied by other men of the family, and sometimes the prospective groom as well, would then call upon the father of the prospec- tive bride and begin the discussion. The men would talk about their families, their reputations, the characteristics of their children before the father of the prospective groom would breech the question about marriage. Should the girl's father agree to the wedding proposal, rounds of coffee would be served to signify the agreement had been made.

Once the agreement had been made between the two families, the family of the groom would host an engagement party. The entire local community would be invited and congratulations would be given. The family of the groom would take one room of the house to receive the guests, while the family of the bride would take another room to receive the guests separately. No large meal was served, but cakes and other sweets would be available along with fresh fruit juices, coffee, and tea. In more recent years cigarettes have been added to the offerings. These are passed around to the guests by younger brothers or cousins of the groom, who are kept busy making sure all of the guests have something to eat or drink. In some instances the engagement was and is still formalized by what is called in Islam "writing the book." This is the formal written agreement between the bride and groom witnessed before an Islamic judge. In all practical purposes the signing of the agreement marries the two. To break the engagement formalized in this way requires the same procedure as divorce in Islamic law. Often the "writing the book" was held off until much closer to the actual wedding celebration.

Preparations for the wedding mobilized both families; the bride and her family had to make her wedding clothes as well as bring what is known as the *jihaz,* all of the things she would need for her own household including furniture. In the past, it could take months of long hours of work to make the heavily embroidered dresses she would wear at her wedding or would take with her to her new home. All the able women in her family would be engaged in helping embroider the clothes. Sometimes the sisters of the groom give the bride embroidered items and would make their brother embroidered handkerchiefs. The grooms family was responsible for the wedding celebration itself, making sure everyone who needed to be included was invited, preparing the wedding meals, hiring musicians, hiring tents if need be, and making sure there was a large enough place to hold the wedding. The cost of the wedding celebration was and is yet today the responsibility of the groom's family.

As the wedding day came closer both families concentrated on the preparations and this often took on a party-like atmosphere with singing and dancing, especially among the women of the families. The songs that were traditionally sung told of the strength of the groom and praised the beauty of the bride, cultural ideals of a proper young couple.

Traditional wedding celebrations often took up to one full week beginning with small gatherings of the family and close friends of the groom or bride in their parents' homes or in tents set up near the houses. These first gatherings often did not include a full meal, but fruit, sweets, juices, and tea. There was singing and dancing, with mainly the young being involved. As the actual wedding day grew closer, each night the parties increased in the number of people invited and the amount of food served while the activities concentrated on the preparations. The night before the wedding day women held a *henna* party where the bride's hands and feet were decorated with designs made with a paste made from the *henna* plant. In Jordan village brides did not have the intricate patterns done associated with the Gulf countries and India, but were often large dot on the palms of the hands and the bottom of the feet similar to those of Bedouin brides. While the bride is being *hennaed* the other women sang songs about married life, the virtues of a husband, and other wedding topics. While the bride was *hennaed* the night before the wedding celebration, the groom's friends would take him the morning of the celebration to the bathhouse for a total scrubbing and a shave. While this was being done his friends would sing and tell jokes.

Once both the bride and groom were dressed and made ready, their friends and relatives would accompany them to the home of the groom's parents. In the past the bride and groom would ride horses and each family would follow singing and clapping. Today the procession for the bride is still done, but by car and truck. All of the horns are beeped and the passengers are singing and clapping. While the groom's friends may still take him to the bathhouse, it is less done today, unless the family itself wants a full traditional wedding.

In Jordan, unlike in some of the nearby countries, village men and women still prefer to sit in segregated groups; often the men sit outside in front of the groom's parents house, and the women, inside the house. Young men sing and dance while the older men usually look on and use the occasion to catch up with local news. Women have their own party inside the house, attending to the bride and giving her advice. They may also sing and dance or watch the young men dance through the windows. Cakes, pastries, candies, tea, coffee, and today cigarettes are served continuously by the groom and his male relatives making sure that everyone is taken care of. As the groom becomes more and more busy as the day wears on the duty falls more and more to his younger brothers. Around noon a main meal will be served which traditionally was *mansif*. Once the meal has been served, the bride is brought to the room where the groom is waiting and in the past the wedding celebration did not end until the bride's virginity had been acknowledged by showing a bloodied white cloth or her underwear. It was the women of the families who did this often placing the bloodied cloth on a basket tray and parading it around to show all of the guests. The woman carrying the tray would be accompanied by the other women of the two families singing and clapping.

Today many weddings have adapted to the new lifestyle in cities such as 'Amman and few families have the time and money for the week-long traditional wedding, even in the countryside. Jordanian weddings have taken on the usual combination Western and Arab format found in many Arab countries of the region. The bride wears a very Western-styled white dress and the wealthier may have them made in Europe. The groom wears a Western-styled formal suit, often black in color. The bride's family still takes her to the wedding celebration in a procession of cars, but instead of the house of the groom's parents, it is often a special wedding hall or the banquet hall of a large hotel. Instead of the segregated seating found even today in Bedouin or village weddings, the guests sit at dining tables in family grouping. Few urban Jordanians would think of displaying the bride's underwear, but even contemporary weddings may end in immediate divorce if the bride is not a virgin.

CONCLUSION

Jordanians have had to make a number of concessions to the rapid economic changes that have occurred since the 1940s. While remaining a deeply conservative society, they have modified many of their traditions without losing their important values. Both men and women have become much better educated, and Jordanians are among of best educated population in the Middle East. Women have increasingly been integrated into the job market in a wide variety of fields without the loss of personal and family honor.

Marriage traditions are maintained by those who can afford the week-long celebrations, but few families can do this today. Increasingly Jordanians have adopted the less elaborate weddings similar to most other urban Arabs in the Middle East—a mix of tradition with borrowings from the west. The cost of even the modified version is so high that some Jordanian men with lower incomes may have to wait until their mid-30s to marry saving money to pay for their wedding. Weddings are still important social markers for families where they can display important social values such as generosity and hospitality.

7

Social Customs and Lifestyle

Jordanians have preserved a good deal of their traditional cultural values even if many of the specific customs have undergone great change in the past fifty years. Jordanians have become a largely urban and middle class society since the end of the 1940s. They have changed from rural villagers and Bedouin to become one of the most highly educated urban populations in the entire Middle East. Despite the impact of these rapid economic and social changes, Jordanians have remained conservative in their world view. An outside observer is immediately struck by the modernity of life in a city like 'Amman, as well as the deep respect Jordanians have for their own cultural values and heritage.

HONOR AND SHAME

The concepts of honor and shame have been greatly overstated in a number of studies of not only Jordan but of the entire Mediterranean region; however, honor and shame are important elements and are measures of a good or bad family. Honor is a collective for an entire group of related people, not only of a single individual. The same can be said of shame; a shameful act will taint an entire group of people and impact possible future relations with other families.

There are several types of honor when the topic is discussed in Arabic and different terms are used. When speaking of the public honor of an extended family or large lineage the term 'ird is used. Such honor is touched when comments are made by others about the behavior of especially the women of the family or lineage. To cast doubt on their honor can result in a "blackening" of the entire family's name. When the name has been blackened it has to be "whitened" and in some instances it can only be whitened by blood.

Honor crimes, where a girl or boy is severely punished for damaging the honor of a family, are not common, but they do sometimes still occur among rural Jordanians. Honor crimes may require even the death of the young person who acted in such a way as to blacken the family's honor. This is most often by behaving immorally, such as having sex out of marriage or even just the rumor of such an action. The family can put this right only by punishing the persons so charged, and the severest punishment is usually reserved for the girl. Her father, brothers, and uncles are responsible for the punishment, which on rare occasions means that she is killed by them.

Jordan is one of the few countries in the Mediterranean that has brought the issue of honor crime into public debate. While it does occur in a number of countries in the Mediterranean including Spain, Italy, and Greece, Jordan has confronted the practice enacting harsher laws for the men involved. As a result of bringing honor crime into public scrutiny, many people have mistakenly concluded that it is a bigger issue in Jordan than in other Mediterranean countries. Instead one should understand that Jordanians' willingness to deal with the matter means that they are among the few who are trying to bring such practices to an end.

In learning what is right and wrong Jordanian children are told that something is good, *zayn* or that it is a shame, *'ayb.* Any action or thought that can bring shame on the family is usually called *'ayb;* it is used to teach children both in the privacy of the home or in public places. Children may not need any other form of correction other than to be told *'ayb* by an adult or even an older child. In addition to *'ayb* children learn that to transgress basic cultural norms is a larger mistake because it is *hasham. Hasham* involves those social norms touching on *'ird,* sex and the honor of women, for which punishment is far more severe. The respect Jordanians have for these important social norms is among the major reasons why they are a conservative people (Muslims and Christians), not because the official government system enforces strict rules of social interaction, but because Jordanians themselves respect them.

Recent changes in the economics, the educational levels, and the subsequent social interactions between men and women have meant that some of the very strict rules that would have applied in the more rural settings of the past cannot be applied in a city like 'Amman. In the rural areas and among the Bedouin interactions between women of a family and a stranger are limited and may require a male chaperone. Today in the workplace, especially in the cities, this is not possible; women will come into contact with men who are not from their families and whom they do not know. Interaction between them means that social distances need to be maintained and some Jordanian

Muslim women have adopted wearing what is called Islamic dress in one form or another to help enforce the social distance. In some businesses it is not unusual to find certain offices are nearly all women while others are nearly all male employees. Female employees will take lunch with other women from the office or nearby offices while men do the same.

During the decades of the 1970s and 1980s more and more Jordanian women came into the job market at nearly all levels. They were needed to replace men who found better paying jobs in Saudi Arabia and the Gulf countries where their high levels of education were needed. Jordanian families overcame their reluctance to allow their daughters, sisters, and wives to work as they filled important jobs. Economic necessity helped overcome custom and today Jordanian women account for around 25 percent of the total work force in the country. Nonetheless, it has been done in such a way as to not damage the honor of the women and their families; for example, women taxi drivers who only take female passengers or "family wings" of restaurants (found in many Islamic countries) where single women (and families) may eat without being looked at by strange men.

RESPECT

Another cultural value closely connected to that of honor is respect. Respect begins within the family, and children are taught to show respect to their parents, grandparents, and older family members. Until recently, a well-behaved child would be expected to greet his or her parents, especially their father, by kissing his hand then touching their forehead with his hand. No matter the age of the child, fathers in particular were to be shown great respect in both the privacy of the home and in public.

One of the measures of a good family was observing the respect shown to older family members by the young. Public respect was also to be demonstrated between younger members of society with anyone older. Children were taught to speak politely to strangers and to refer to anyone older as uncle or aunt. Well behaved Jordanian children still use the family terms of uncle or aunt when addressing an elder person, but very few families still insist on kissing their hands.

VISITING FAMILY AND FRIENDS

Jordan is a strongly family-oriented society and among the social customs still conformed to today is that of visiting family and friends. It is considered a necessity to visit as a means to keep families together as well as an important means to demonstrate friendships. Certain days of the week, such as Fridays for Muslims and Sundays for Christians, often include large meals at the home of the family patriarch or at least at a relative's house after the noon prayer or morning mass. The month of Ramadan is marked by frequent visits between households and sharing breaking the day's fast. The first week of Ramadan, Jordanians tend to visit mainly the homes of relatives while during the other three weeks they often visit the homes of friends.

Visiting has its social rules and the guest/host relationship is an important feature of the culture. For both guest and host, there are expectations of behavior, length of stay, and level of hospitality given, depending on the closeness of the relationship between the parties and the purpose of the visit. The visit could be formal, such as to propose marriage or close a business deal, or informal between close friends or relatives. Some of the newer apartment complexes have been built with two entrances for each apartment; one for the family to use and one for guests. Many homes and apartments are built so that the women of the family do not have to come into direct contact with a guest and still go about their normal activities without being seen or having their honor compromised. These special guest rooms are a contemporary form of the traditional guest room or house found in the village architecture (see chapter on architecture). Like the older form, the room is usually one of the more lavishly decorated in the house and can be in traditional or Arab style, where guests are expected to sit on mattresses covered with Bedouin rugs and there is a hearth for the host to prepare Arabic coffee in front of the guest or in European style with a western arrangement of chairs, tables, and couches, and no hearth for coffee.

Food and drink are important features of visiting, even between close friends and family members. For a host to not provide at least fruit, sweets, coffee or tea would be the mark of both bad manners and a poor host. If unexpected guests arrive and a family isn't prepared, then children will be sent to buy things from a nearby store or borrow from a neighbor. Since guests will often drop by unexpectedly, most Jordanian families have a supply of foods and drinks for them. Women are expected to be ready to even make a meal should a guest arrive and be hungry. Guests will be urged to eat and drink by the host who will often repeat phrases such as *ahlan wa sahlan, ya hala' bil-Dayf,* or *tafaddal* meaning "welcome," "welcome to our guest," and "help yourself." Guests are bound to take something. To visit and refuse to eat or to take a coffee or tea would mark a cold relationship and even hostility on the part of the guest.

The guest/host relationship is very important stemming from the rural and Bedouin background of many Jordanians. In the past and even today among the Bedouin, a guest is welcome no matter who he is. A member of an enemy tribe is welcome in the tent of his host and by custom is allowed to remain for three days. Politeness dictates that on the morning of the fourth day the guest will leave and for another three days is protected by his host. The act of providing and accepting food and drink establishes an important bond between the two with understood obligations on the parties. One way of ending problems between families, especially among the Bedouin, is for a meal to be served and both parties invited to participate—to break bread together or in Arabic to eat salt and bread together.

HOSPITALITY AND GENEROSITY

Jordanians take the cultural values of hospitality and generosity seriously and one frequently hears the Arabic greeting *ahlan wa sahlan* or "welcome" wherever one goes in the country. Often the greeting is put in the dual form *ahlayn wa sahlayn* meaning "the visitor is doubly welcome" or with *marhabah* (another word for welcome in Arabic) or even *mi't marhab* "one hundred welcomes" added to the phrase. Another traditional greeting is *ya hala'* or *ya hala' bil-Dayf* (or greetings to our guest). When visiting a Jordanian home the guest will be frequently told he is welcome and urged to eat and have tea, coffee, or juices with *tafaddal* or please partake. Jordan is known as the Land of *Ahlan wa Sahlan*.

Customs of hospitality and generosity are part of the duties of a good host in Arab culture that stretch far back into antiquity. The great pre-Islamic epics tell of the lavish hospitality of tribal leaders and ruling Quraysh clan of Makkah had established a reputation for generosity at the time of the Prophet Muhammad. Present day hospitality and generosity are measured next to the legends of the past, such as those of the Bedouin boy Hatim al-Tayy who in order to feed guests slaughtered his father's camels until not a one was left. Among the Bedouin, poverty of a family when linked to their generosity to guests is greatly admired and no Bedouin leader can maintain his position if he is not both hospitable and generous to whoever comes to his house. Bedouin who have particular reputations for Hatim al-Tayy like generosity are not only greatly admired, but will be pointed out to others during celebrations such as weddings.

Hospitality and generosity are cultural values shared by all Jordanians, but Bedouin often criticize villagers for what they consider to be a lack of both. Villagers will accept Bedouin invitations or will avail themselves of the hospitality of any tent knowing a guest will not be turned away and there will always be a meal or at least tea. However, Bedouin claim the reverse is not always true. Villagers they deal with for summer pasture and water will not invite them into their homes, and their homes are more restricted. Tales of villager miserliness—only two cups of coffee or glasses of tea for example—will be told to illustrate that they are not as virtuous as the Bedouin. While it is true that villagers do not invite people to their homes as often as the Bedouin, they definitely do invite, and in the experience of the author, are just as hospitable and generous to a stranger as the Bedouin. In the recent past, some villages had special guest houses to both house guests overnight and serve as places where the village notables could honor their guests with large meals (see chapter on architecture). In addition the guest would not be in contact with the women of any household and their honor would not be compromised.

Generosity can be taken to extremes by Jordanians who feel it is their responsibility for the guest to leave happy. If a guest admires something in the house, it will be immediately offered as a gift unless in the course of admiring it, the guest invokes the name of God by saying something like *Ma Sha' Allah* (what God wills) and makes it clear that its place is in the house of the host. The hospitality and generosity of many rural Jordanians, especially the Bedouin, is frequently abused by tourists who enjoy it without understanding or appreciating the costs they are causing the family. Honor is such that no one will ask for compensation, though in places where tourists have so greatly abused these social customs, people have had to put aside honor and ask for money. The concepts of hospitality and generosity are reciprocal, that is, the host of today is the guest of tomorrow and the hospitality shown a guest will be repaid by someone in the future. If this is not possible, then it is both polite and customary to bring gifts for the host's family. Such gifts can be candies or pastries (sometimes in brought in inlaid wooden boxes from Syria), sets of juice or tea glasses, or coffee cups for Arabic coffee. These will not be opened while the guest is still there, but will be opened later when if they are not liked, no one will know and be hurt.

SOCIAL CLUBS: RELIGIOUS, ETHNIC, AND GENDER SPACES

Among the very important places for community gatherings are social clubs. Some of the social clubs are based on religion or ethnic identity; there are social clubs for example for Orthodox Christians, Armenians, Circassians, Shishans, and Palestinians. These serve important social functions for the communities and can be the focal point of much of their activities.

Social clubs are places where parents can come with their children and oftentimes the clubs provide play spaces, planned activities for the children, and perhaps even a swimming pool. Parents can leave the children at the club or spend time there themselves talking to each other as the children are taken care of by club employees. The clubs are places where women in particular can observe possible future marriage partners for their children and note those who are behaving properly and those who are not. Clubs are also places where young people can mix without there being any sort of problem. The group activities are chaperoned and parents can feel comfortable allowing their children to go even if they are not present.

Some social clubs like those for the Circassians and Armenians have been important means for cultural survival for minorities. The clubs serve as places where minority languages are spoken and where children are taught their own dances, songs, celebrate national holidays and events, and encouraged to wear national dress at such events. In recent years the Circassians and Shishans have used such organizations as the main tool for a cultural renaissance where Circassian and Shishan cultural awareness and pride have been revived among the young. Special cultural days have been organized for not only members of the Circassian and Shishan communities, but are open to the general public. Displays of arts, crafts, music, dance, and foods not only help revive cultural awareness among their own young people, but help develop awareness among non-Circassians and Shishans as well. Circassians and Shishans have played important roles in the recent history of Jordan and public activities by their social clubs help highlight their contributions to the country.

One of the most important social clubs is the coffeehouse. The coffeehouse has been until the past few years a male space where men come to read the newspaper, discuss politics, play backgammon or chess as well as to have a Turkish coffee and smoke a water pipe. The coffeehouse has a long tradition in Jordan and the nearby countries, dating back as far as perhaps the Mamluk period. Before coffee was discovered by a wandering Sufi mystic in Ethiopia, such places were teahouses and served not only as important male spaces, but also as places of business. It was a better place to discuss the details of a business agreement with a more relaxed atmosphere. Entertainment was often part of the experience and professional storytellers were employed by the owners of such businesses to recite popular tales, such as that of the great pre-Islamic Bedouin hero Antar bin Shadad, the tragic love story of Qays and Layla, the Bedouin hero Abu Zayd al-Hilali, or the Mamluk Sultan Baybars al-Bunduqdari. When the radio was introduced most of the storytellers lost their trade, though there are still a few coffeehouses in al-Zarqa', Jordan and Damascus where traditional storytelling is an evening feature. Today the radio has been replaced by the TV but the general purpose of the establishment is the same: a men's club often patronized by the men of the neighborhood.

Jordan is the first Arab country to have an all women's coffeehouse. Based on the same principles as that of the traditional male coffeehouse, the one for women offers tea, coffee, games, and heated political discussion. The success of the all women's coffeehouse in 'Amman may spark similar ones in Jordan or other parts of the Arab world where career women also want some form of relaxation away from the house.

EMERGENCE OF THE MIDDLE CLASS

Since the 1960s more and more Jordanians have become urban and middle class. The percentage of Jordanians who have a minimum of a high school diploma and who work in the service sector or in white collar jobs has greatly increased. Unlike many other countries in the region, Jordan has a fairly large middle class. While most have tried to maintain the core values of their more rural origins, nonetheless, the changes in their economic and educational levels has meant that they have had to adjust their lifestyles.

The optimal age for marriage has risen for both men and women as a result of the rise in educational levels. Many postpone making marriage plans until they have finished university or post high school vocational training. Men want to establish themselves in a job with a good salary before thinking seriously about marriage. Women too want to finish their education before being tied down with a husband and family, and more and more agree to marriage only if they are going to be allowed to work. Muslim Jordanian women take advantage of the need for a marriage contract and will stipulate clauses such as right to work.

Many Jordanians attend universities inside Jordan or abroad and among the new ideal quality for a good bride is one who has a university degree. Some marriages are dependent upon the bride to be completing her BA degree within a specific number of years indicating no failed courses. Educated wives are seen as better as they are better partners in life being able to understand the work pressures of their husbands. They are expected to be better mothers because they can understand medical care and nutrition better than an uneducated woman as well as help the children with their homework. Educated wives may also have careers that can be a great help to the overall income for the family.

MIDDLE-CLASS VALUES AND TRADITIONAL VALUES

The growth of a new middle class has brought younger Jordanians into conflict with some of the older traditional social customs. Many of these focus on the family, children, and women's place within family and society.

The Jordanian family is changing from the rural ideal of a large number of children to the smaller, western model of two to three children. Both men and women tend to marry later than their parents and grandparents, reducing the number of years a married woman is able to have children. There are still pressures from the older members of their families to have children as soon after marriage as possible; a woman who is not pregnant within the first year of marriage was the subject of gossip in the past, but many younger Jordanians are making the choice to postpone having children and space them out. Women may not have a child until several years after being married especially if she has her own work career.

Career women are a relatively new idea in Jordanian society. It is not to say that in the past women were not involved in owning and managing businesses. The Ottoman court records in Damascus have numerous references to major businesses owned and managed by women, but they were for the most part wealthy urban women. For most Jordanians, women were the managers of houses, while men were the bread winners. Women remained at home until the shock of the first Arab-Israeli War drove thousands of Palestinians into refugee camps and women had to work for the daily survival of their families. Jordanian women took to the job market when Jordanian men were recruited for middle- and high-level management positions in the Gulf States and Saudi Arabia. As late as 1982 Jordanian families refused to let their daughters and wives work in positions such as waitresses or airline hostesses.

Jordanian women were greatly helped by the examples of the Royal women. The wives and daughters of King Hussein were involved in numerous social and educational programs highlighting the need for all Jordanians to be educated and the right for women to choose a career. Jordanian women entered schools of science and engineering where many have excelled. Jordanian women are studying not only in local institutions of higher education, but in Europe, North America, and Asia. The high profile of the Jordanian royal women has been important role models for all Jordanian women.

CONCLUSION

Despite the changes to the family size and the greater role for women in the economy, traditional values are strong. The changes that have occurred have not so far changed the way people think about their values—or passing these values on to their children. The basic core values such as honor, respect, hospitality, and generosity are still part of all Jordanians.

8

Music and Dance

Traditional music and dances in Jordan are mainly those of the rural populations: villagers and Bedouin. Most musicologists would classify them as folk meaning that they are not the sophisticated music and dance found in such centers of high Arab culture as Damascus, Aleppo, Baghdad, or Cairo, but a more rustic music produced more by gifted amateurs rather than trained professionals. However, the roots of the more sophisticated music of high Arab and Islamic culture are in the music of the Bedouin. In addition, many village performers were exposed to the refined tastes of urban professionals even in the past. Jordanians have been linked closely to important cultural centers such as Damascus for millennia. Jordan's desert was a favorite retreat for the Umayyad princes who organized lavish parties that always included music and dance. Other ruling dynasties have left a lasting influence on local music, most notably the Ottomans.

Arabic music has several major roots: pre-Islamic Arabia and Persia, as well as Classical Greece. Each of these has contributed to the set of modal scales or *maqamat* used and eventually eight different modal scales were established along with a large number of sub-modal scales between the ninth to tenth centuries A.D. in Damascus, Baghdad, and Cordoba, major centers of Arabic culture at the time. The development of Arabic music took several centuries starting under the patronage of the Umayyad rulers in Damascus and later the 'Abbasids in Baghdad and the Umayyads in Cordoba. Inclusion of numerous ethnicities in the expanding Arab-Islamic empires allowed direct contact between different traditions from India and Central Asia to Spain. Systems of musical notations and instruments were introduced and modified into the Arabic music of today.

As noted above, an array of new musical instruments were introduced, developed, and refined. The Arabs already had a wide range of drums made with wooden or ceramic bodies with one or two heads of animal hide or fish skin. End-blown cane flutes were the main wind instruments, along with the several types of reed instruments. Of the string instruments, the Arabs developed the one-stringed fiddle or *rabab,* the lyre or *simsimiyah,* and the *'ud* or lute (the word "lute" is derived from the Arabic *al-'ud*). Other instruments were borrowed from the ancient civilizations of Mesopotamia, Egypt, Anatolia, Persia, and the Indus valley. Since the nineteenth century a number of western instruments have been adopted to Arabic music such as the violin, piano, saxophone, trumpet, and most recently the electric organ, guitar, and synthesizer.

BEDOUIN MUSIC AND DANCE

The Bedouin music is one of the primary sources for Arab and Islamic musical forms. Bedouin music was and is primarily vocal and instruments, when used, are there to assist the voice or fill the void while the singer takes a breath, speaks to the audience, or composes the next set of verses. Bedouin love poetry and the better singers are also the better poets. That is, the voice, while important, may not sound musical to an outsider, but for the Bedouin listening, the skill to improvise and produce a new poem, even if based on an existing format, is what makes the singer good.

There are a number of different types of poetry which are also considered to be types of music. The type of poem, long epic (*qasidah*) or short love poem (*ghazal*) or even shorter haiku-like social criticism poem (*ghinwiyah*), influence how they are sung, the number of people singing, use of refrain, and whether or not it has instrumental accompaniment. Many Bedouin songs are without any accompaniment other than clapping hands or one-sided drums. The rhythms used reflect those of Bedouin life such as the pace of a riding camel.

Bedouin use few musical instruments but the *rabab* or *rababah* is essential to the recitation of poetry (see chapter on literature). The *rabab* is oftentimes called *rabab al-sha'ir* or the poet's *rabab*. The instrument is simple and easy to make being a shallow square sound box covered in skin with a long, thin round stick to form the neck. There is only one string made of horse hair or animal gut and the instrument is played with a bow, again simply made from a bent stick with horse hair to make the string. There are no frets on the neck, which allows a skilled player a large range of notes despite the fact it has only one string. The *rabab* may sound off-key when first heard by someone not used to it, but its low tones go well with the flow of epic poetry and forms a soothing background for the listeners. In contemporary performances the *rabab* may be replaced by a violin, but it might be played as if it were a *rabab* resting on the player's leg rather than being held under the chin and bowed in the same fashion as a cello.

Most Bedouin music is vocal and it would be rare to hear something that was only instrumental. Instrumental music is more or less confined to that of shepherds playing flutes to pass the time. Songs frequently employ a limited range of notes and those for celebrations are for a group; solos are not common other than to sing a verse for a call and response format. Songs are accompanied by clapping, which can produce complicated, syncopated rhythms, and large round one-sided hand drums called *tar*s. It is rare that men and women sing or dance together, but at celebrations such as weddings women and men may engage in call and response songs between them, though they do not sit together.

There are a number of different dances performed by the Bedouin, and like the music, there is little mixing between men and women. Most dances are for celebrations, especially weddings, and most men's dances are line dances of one kind or another. Men take their places in long straight lines standing shoulder to shoulder. In front of the line there are several lead dancers, and in some Bedouin dances, the leader can be a woman. When the leaders are men they move back and forth in front of the line using their robes or *bisht*s like giant bird wings—it is supposed to imitate the movements of an eagle. The men in the line clap in time with the movements of the leaders and their own upper body movements, as they chant in unison a breathy "a-hee." When a woman leads such dances she often brandishes a sword which she uses to signal the men in the line to follow her commands: stand, bend, move right, and so forth. The dance becomes faster and more and more frenzied until the leaders indicate that it is over by dropping the sleeves of their *bisht*s or the sword down to their sides.

Another popular men's line dance is the *dabkah,* where again the men line up shoulder to shoulder or place their arms on the shoulders of the men next to them. In the *dabkah* the line moves, often in a circle, using specific steps punctuated with stomps and kicks. Bedouin forms of *dabkah* tend to be less complicated than those of the villagers with fewer variations of steps or step patterns. *Dabkah* requires using some musical instruments, mainly a drum, usually made of ceramic with either fish skin or leather head, called a *darabukah* and a cane or metal end blown flute called a *nay.* Women also perform *dabkah* standing closely together and holding each others' hands. The movements are restrained and dignified allowing their dresses to swing and sway gracefully indicating the steps.

Village Music and Dance

Village music and dance is greatly influenced by both Bedouin traditions and urban high-art traditions. Village musicians employ a much wider variety of musical instruments than the Bedouin, and they rarely play the *rabab*. The more traditional and rustic instruments, such as some of the reed wind instruments such as the *mizmar,* are sometimes replaced today with electric organs attempting to make a similar sound.

Villagers have long been exposed to the urban traditions of small, chamber-like orchestras, which until the early twentieth century performed in urban coffeehouses and even some of the better bathhouses or *hamam*s. The orchestra played instrumental music or included at least one singer capable of singing popular or art songs. The orchestras were composed of around five or six musicians who played the *darabukah,* the *riqq* (or tambourine), the *kaman* or *kamanjah* (or violin), the *nay* (or cane flute), and the *qanun* (or plucked zither). Among the types of late Ottoman music that such musical groups performed was the *basharf,* which is the Arabic version of the Turkish word *pesrev,* originally an instrumental prelude to a longer sung piece. Other forms borrowed into village music from urban art music are *muwashshahat* (originally from Muslim Spain) and *qadud al-Halabiyah* (a Syrian form similar to the *muwashshahat*). These later two used colloquial Arabic in part if not all of the words. A popular musical poetic form is the *zajal* (see the chapter on literature) which is usually in colloquial Arabic. *Zajal* is often sung by two opposing sides with the poets improvising lines which their side then sings as a chorus. Such songs are usually accompanied by some one playing the *darabukah* and perhaps an *'ud* or a long necked variety with metal strings called a *buzuk,* similar to the Greek bouzouki.

Like the Bedouin, village men and women traditionally did not sit together to sing or listen to music. Both entertained themselves even during important celebrations. Men and women would gather in different places, or if in the same house, in different rooms. Women were less proficient in playing musical instruments and for the most part used only drums with their songs. Women did not engage in the same kinds of songs to display the poetic skills that men did, but nonetheless, their songs are equally important. Many songs tell of their lives, both the good and the bad, as well as give advice to the younger women. Women used a number of devises, such as comedy, to illustrate or to give deeper meanings to the listeners. Unlike Bedouin women who have a wide audience for their songs of criticism, traditionally village women were confined to speaking to each other.

Village dances were and still are line dances. Line dances are found throughout the eastern Mediterranean from the Balkans on the west, to Iraq on the east, and Sinai and Jordan on the south. In most of the Arab countries the dance is called *dabkah* and it varies somewhat from place to place; it is possible for the trained eye to know if the dance being performed is Syrian, Lebanese, Palestinian, or Jordanian. The Bedouin in

Jordan have a slow and stately form of the dance, while the villagers have a number of different steps, some of which are rapid and highly complicated combinations of stomps and kicks. Similar to the Bedouin, most village *dabkah* is accompanied by the *darabukah* and the *nay,* or the large double sided drum called *tabl* and the reed instrument similar to an oboe called *mizmar.*

Similar to the Bedouin *dabkah,* in village forms of the line dance men place their arms over the shoulders of their neighbors and follow instructions given by the dance leader who is positioned in front of the line. The leader holds a short stick, which he uses to help send specific messages to the rest of the dancers. By holding it in a certain way, the other dancers know what steps are coming up so that the whole group stays together. The leader's signals are also read by the drummer and flute player who know how to change the music if need be. Some dance leaders use highly decorated sticks covered in woolen braid and tassels. Others may prefer to use an embroidered handkerchief which has beaded tassels at each of the four corners that he will spin in the air as he calls the steps. Jordanian *dabkah* differs from those around it by certain steps, such as one where the dancers do a number of very quick kicks in succession, usually five, while in place followed by a single stomp step.

Women have their own *dabkah* and for men and women to be in the same line while dancing is a recent change and an influence from professional Palestinian, Lebanese, and Syrian folk troupes. Traditionally village women did not dance with the men, but separately either in their own space or interspersed between men's dances. The women join hands and move in a slow stately manner in a large circle. The leader takes her place at the head of the line and the others follow her movements and steps. Similar to Bedouin women, the movements of the dancers' dresses give the dance an air of dignity and calm.

For weddings in particular, women have other dances that they perform only for each other. These are folk versions of the better known cabaret dance called Belly Dance in the west, but *raqs baladi* (local dance) or *raqs sharqi* (eastern dance) in the Middle East. Women move their shoulders and hips to the beat of drums. In the past, these dances were used to help educate a bride on her sexual duties, thus the songs women sing while others dance are filled with innuendo and double meaning, causing great laughter among the women. Unlike the more familiar cabaret form of the dance, women do not wear suggestive clothing other than to tie a scarf around their hips or waists to accentuate that part of the body. Until the early twentieth century wealthier rural elite would hire professional all-female music groups from the cities to entertain the women during their nightly parties leading up to a wedding.

The women who performed in such groups were not highly respected since such professions caused them to lose much of their honor and they were classified by most with prostitutes.

Circassians and Shishans

The Circassians and Shishans preserved their music and dance traditions, and in the past several decades they have actively promoted them among their own youth. Their music and dance traditions differ greatly from those of their Arab neighbors coming from the Caucasus Mountains between Turkey, Iran, and Russia. Their music has more in common with that of Iran and Turkish-speaking Azerbaijan than with the Arabs.

Circassian and Shishan music does have the same modal base as that of the Arabs, but owes its interpretation to that of the Turks and Persians. The singing voice is important, as it is with the Arabs, but the style favors greater use of melismatic passages and higher octaves similar to Persian and Turkish traditions. The rhythms used also are similar to Turkish and Persian ones using more of the player's fingers striking the drum head individually rather than with the more open-hand Arab method.

More traditional musical instruments have been to a great extent replaced by the accordion. While older string instruments such as the *saz,* a long necked lute with several sympathetic drone strings, and soft sounding reed instruments such as the *duduk* are still played, the accordion has come to dominate dance music. The accordion is accompanied by several types of drums, most very similar to those used by the Arabs though the more traditional form of the Circassian version of the *darabukah* is made of wood and not ceramic, giving the sound a more rounded tone rather than the crisp sound of the Arab drum. Circassians also use the large round hand drum or *tar,* though theirs has a narrower body and can be even larger in diameter.

Circassian and Shishan dance has much in common with ballet. The men dance on the tips of their toes making graceful walking-like steps. With their Cossack-like dress and high leather boots they are a striking figure dancing on their toes. The men use their arms and hands while dancing much again like a ballet dancer. In some Circassian dances men throw their daggers high into the air and catch them as they come plunging down. Men and women dance together in pairs and the women's movements are barely discernable. She seems to glide effortlessly across the floor with no evidence that her feet are moving. Her floor-length dress makes no sign that her feet and legs are in motion, and her upper body and head stay perfectly straight and steady.

Contemporary Music

Jordan has not been an important center of Arab music but Jordanians are avid consumers of it. From the end of World War I until the middle of the 1970s most of the popular music in the Arab world came from two major sources, Egypt and Syria. Egypt, and Cairo in particular, was the cultural capital of the Arab world, whose singers such as Umm Kalthum are listened to throughout the Arab world and beyond, even today. Those who wanted to have careers in music came to Cairo. The Syrians Farid al-Atrash and his sister Asmahan, the Lebanese Sabah, and even the Algerian Wardah al-Jaza'iriyah all went to Cairo and sang in the Egyptian dialect. Starting in the 1950s Beirut also was able to assert its influence in the Arab world. Both Beirut and Damascus had recording studios as early as the 1890s, but distribution of their music was limited. Lebanese and Syrians began to produce popular hits using their dialects of Arabic, and in the 1960s stars such as Fairuz and Wadi' al-Safi could compete with the Egyptian stars such as Abd al-Halim Hafiz and Najat al-Saghirah. In the 1960s Jordanian music was represented by the Bedouin star Samirah Tawfiq, who sang more rustic sounding songs in the Bedouin dialect. Her music became popular throughout the Arab world and was identified as Jordanian, though she was not. At the same time Syrian music made itself felt with singers such as Sabah al-Fakhri and Fahd Balan.

Saudi and Gulf Arab music first entered into the mainstream of popular Arab music in 1976 when Talal Madah's song "Magadir" became an international (international being within the Arab world) hit. His success was followed by other Saudi singers such as Muhammad 'Abduh. Saudi and Gulf music remains popular today, but in the early 1980s the new Cairo pop sound called *Jil* (or new generation music) exploded onto the music scene with the Egyptian Nubian singer Muhammad Munir. The new Cairo sound was quickly adopted by younger Lebanese singers and a Cairo-Beirut connection was established that still exists today.

In 1990 Algerian Rai music was able to have its first pan-Arab hit with the song "Didi" by Shab Khalid. Most Jordanians had a hard time at first understanding the Algerian dialect or the political and social criticisms in the music, but today other Algerian and Franco-Algerian singers such as Shab Mami and Rachid Taha are well known in the Arab east. August of 1990 also marked the start of the first Gulf War between Iraq and the United States with Iraq's invasion of Kuwait. Many Jordanians did not support the United States decision to militarily force Iraq out of Kuwait. Although Jordanians were familiar with Iraqi music and singers such as Sa'adun al-Jabir since the 1970s, the war seemed to spark an even greater interest in it.

After the United States invasion of Iraq in 2003 Iraqi music became even more popular with the Jordanian public.

Today young Jordanian singers have a range of styles to choose from. Some may wish to be traditional while others prefer the Cairo-Pop *Jil* style. Others have begun to sing Iraqi songs, especially *chobe,* the Iraqi line dance similar to the *dabkah.* Jordan has a number of locally known artists, but few Jordanians have broken into the larger Arab market. There are local recording studios, and on local television it is possible to see their music videos, but few have gone on to stardom in Beirut or Cairo, which remain the two most important centers for Arab music.

CONCLUSION

Jordanian music and dance has long been that of rural people. Jordan's ties to urban centers such as Damascus did influence Jordanian musicians and singers, but the conservative nature of the population meant that its influence was limited. There were few Jordanians who could patronize a professional class of musicians and singers, thus most of the music and dance performed were for special occasions and performed by gifted amateurs. While the poetic forms were highly developed, especially by the Bedouin, sophisticated art music and dance remained an urban art associated with Damascus, Cairo, and Baghdad.

The introduction of diverse music styles increased with the increase in broadcast media after World War I. Radio and films brought the popular and classical forms of music from mainly Cairo at first. The increase in local broadcasting stations from countries like Lebanon and Syria gave rise to a pride in the similar musical traditions of Greater Syria among Jordanians. With television Jordan was opened up to even greater influences, and clearly some have been politically motivated. As noted above, Iraqi music had been known for some time before young Jordanians began to produce it themselves following the American invasion in 2003. Popularity of Lebanese singers such as Fairuz and the Palestinian Marcel Khalifah has much to do with the politics of the 1960s to the 1990s in the Arab world. Today Jordanians are familiar with nearly every form of Arab music from the most traditional to the new forms of Arabic rap.

Glossary

‘Abayah   Another name for a Bisht.

Ablaq   Alternating layers of black basalt and white limestone building stones; architectural style developed by the Mamluks for major urban monuments and used by peasants in southern Syria, Jordan, Lebanon, and Palestine where the natural rock is available.

Abu   Arabic for father; used in honorific title such as Abu Muhammad noting the first born male child in a family.

Adab   Literature; manners.

Adhan   Call to prayer.

Adib   A well educated and mannered person.

Ahlan wa Sahlan   Welcome; Jordanians use the phrase so often that the country is called the "Land of Ahlan wa Sahlan."

Al-Mahram   The closed, family, women's side of the tent.

Al-Shigg   The public, men's side of the tent.

Amir   Prince; under the Mamluks the term was applied to the highest ranking military commanders.

‘Aqil   Intelligence; among the Shi'ites it refers to the Cosmic Intelligence.

‘Arjah   A highly decorated headpiece worn by village and Bedouin women in southern Syria and northern Jordan.

‘Asabah   Headband worn by women; in Jordan it is often made of brocade cloth from Homs, highly colorful floral cottons; or a man's shimagh.

Asawir Shirkaz   Circassian bracelets. A type of jewelry introduced by the Circassians and Shishans; nielloed work on silver.

‘Ashurah   The 10th Day of the first Islamic month. Among Sunnis it is a children's festival while for Shi'ites it marks the death of Imam Hussein.

Asil   Pure; term is used to designate those Bedouin tribes whose economy used to be based on raising camels. It is also used to refer to purebred horses or camels.

'Asr   Mid-afternoon prayer.

Atabek   Turkish term and a title given to high dignitaries under the Saljuqs and other Turkish dynasties.

Awlad   Sons of as in the tribal name Awlad 'Ali.

'Ayb   Shame; shame on you.

'Ayn   Arabic word for eye as well as for a natural spring.

'Ayn al-Hasud   Evil eye or eye of envy; believed can cause great harm if attracted by too much praise.

Badiyah   Desert that can be lived in most of the year such as Badiyat al-Sham.

Badu   The Arabic plural for Bedouin—singular is Badawi.

Bani   Sons of as in the tribal name Bani Khalid or Bani Sakhr.

Barakah   Blessings; usually in reference to divine blessing.

Bashraf (Pesrev)   An instrumental introduction to a much longer musical piece in classical Arabic and Turkish music. The word is the Arabic form of the original Turkish word, Pesrev.

Bayram   Turkish term for festival, feast. *See also* 'Id.

Bayt   House, home, household.

Bayt Hajar   Literally "House of Stone"; term used by Bedouin for the permanent dwellings built by villagers.

Bayt Sha'r   Literally "House of Hair"; the black, goat hair Bedouin tent.

Bisht   Large outer cloak worn by men.

Buzuk   Long necked lute with metal strings similar to the Greek bouzouki.

Chobe   Popular line dance in Iraq very similar to the dabkah.

Dabkah   Popular line dance in Jordan, Palestine, Lebanon, and Syria.

Darabukah   Single headed cylinder drum made of metal or ceramic.

Dar al-Kursi   Literally "Throne House"; term used to refer to the large village and urban homes with an upper story guest room.

Dishdashah   Ankle-length shirt worn by men in the Middle East.

Duduk   Soft, mellow sounding reed instrument used by the Circassians and Shishans.

Duhur   Mid-day prayer.

Fajr   Dawn prayer.

Farw   Pelt; winter coat worn by Bedouin men made of several sheep pelts sewn together to make a coat.

Fath   Literally opening or victory; al-Fath is the name of the Palestinian organization founded by Yasir 'Arafat and has come to dominate the Palestinian Liberation Organization (PLO).

Fazah or Wastayn   Tent with two main poles.

Fusha   Classical or Standard Arabic; based on the Qu'ran and the conventions of written, literary Arabic.

Gatbah   One-poled tent.

Ghazal   Love poem.

Ghinnawi   Short poem or song most often used to make social or political comment.

Habak   Herringbone stitch; frequently used stitch in weaving and in clothing.

Hadar   Arabic designation for settled peoples, especially villagers.

Hadith   Sayings of the Prophet Muhammad; one of the five major sources for Islamic law.

Haj   Pilgrimage; the once in a lifetime pilgrimage made by Muslims to Mecca.

Hammam   Turkish bath.

Hasham   Shame.

Henna   The leaves of the plant are ground into a powder and when mixed with water becomes a paste used to decorate hands and feet of women for special occasions.

Hijab   Charm or talisman; also the term for the scarf or veil worn by many Muslim women.

Hilf   "Ally"; term used for the association between Bedouin tribes of equal status.

Hosh   Courtyard.

Ibn 'Amm   First cousin on the paternal side; traditionally the preferred marriage partner for a young woman.

'Id   Holiday, festival, feast.

'Id al-Adha (Bayram Qurban)   Literally "of the Sacrifice"; festival that marks the closure of the Haj rituals.

'Id al-Fitr   Literally "of Breaking the Fast"; the festival that marks the end of Ramadan.

Ijma'   Consensus; one of the five major sources of Islamic law.

Ikhwan   Brothers; often applied to mean brotherhood

Imam   In Sunni Islam the term is applied to any one who leads prayer; in Shi'i Islam the term is used for those who were accepted as the head of the community. For most of the Shi'i today there have been 12 Imams and they are expecting the return of the 12th.

Intifadah   Uprising; term used to describe the recent conflict between the Palestinians in the occupied territories and the Israeli authorities.

'Ird   Public honor of a family or tribe.

'Ishiyah   Night prayer.

Jabal   Mountain.

Jamid   Hard type of yogurt; made by adding salt to cause the yogurt to dry.

Jazirah   Island.

Jihaz   The household materials brought to a newly weds home by the bride.

Jil   Literally "generation"; the name for a type of popular Egyptian music also called Cairo Pop.

Jinn   Genie; spirits mentioned in the Qu'ran as created from fire and can be both good or evil.

Jund   Military district; one of the administrative divisions used after the Arab conquest of former Byzantine and Sassanid territories.

Kaman, Kamanjah   Terms used for the western type violin that has greatly replaced the rabab.

Khalifah   Caliph; term used for the person who is the earthly successor to the political power and authority of the Prophet Muhammad as head of the entire Muslim community.

Khawah   "Brotherhood" tax imposed on settled peoples or weaker Bedouin tribes by the Asil tribes.

Khirqah   Traditional headcloth worn by village women in Palestine and Jordan, often highly decorated with embroidery.

Khubz   Bread.

Khubz min al-Tabun   Type of bread baked in a tabun or traditional oven or in hot coals.

Khubz Suri   Syrian bread; pocket bread.

Kuffiyah   Another term for the traditional head cloth worn by men.

Madhhab   School of law in Islam. There are four schools of law in Sunni Islam; Hanbali, Maliki, Hanafi, and Shafi'. Most Jordanians belong to the Shafi' school.

Maghrib   Sunset prayer.

Malikah   Literally "royal"; colorful woman's dress made of green, yellow, and red strips of silk cloth sewn together vertically then embroidered with silk floss and gold or silver metal threads. This type of dress was common in the region of Ma'an in southern Jordan as well as in the Bethlehem area of Palestine.

Mamluk   Arabic term meaning "owned" used for military slaves who replaced dependency on tribal levies. They came to power in Egypt and Syria after the collapse of the Ayyubid dynasty in 1250. Bahri Mamluks ruled from 1250 to 1382 and the Burji Mamluks ruled from 1382 to 1517.

Mansif   National dish of Jordan; half of a sheep or goat severed on a bed of rice and shrak over which a salty yogurt sauce is poured.

Maqam(at)   The term has a number of uses; a place where an important person in Islam is buried; a type of Arabic prose; a musical mode.

Ma'rash   Covered work space in a traditional village courtyard.

Marhabah   Welcome, and another word in Arabic for welcome; the usual response is "Marhabtayn" or "Two Welcomes" or "You are doubly welcome."

Masaharti   The person employed in a neighborhood to announce the last meal of the night before the day's fast begins during Ramadan.

Masriyyah   A type of silver bracelet popular with Bedouin women made in Egypt.

Mastabah   Bench; often built of stone and flanking the entrance to major homes in villages and cities.

Mawlid al-Nabi   The Prophet's Birthday.

Milfa'   *See* Shambar.

Millet   Turkish term from the Arabic millah; a religious community recognized by the Ottoman state as a community and thus allowed to have its own internal regulations with a recognized head responsible to the state.

Mizmar   Traditional double-reed musical instrument frequently used in folk music.

Mthawlath   Tent with three main poles.

Mukhtar   Village headman usually chosen from among the leading families.

Musakhin Jordanian/Palestinian dish made of baked chicken and bread seasoned with sumac.

Musallah Place for prayer; usually the extended areas outside the precinct of a mosque.

Musalsalah Television series.

Mutusarrafiyyah Ottoman period administrative district composed of several *sanjaqs*.

Muwashshahah Type of poetry developed in al-Andalus (Muslim Spain) using both Classical and spoken Arabic set to music.

Nagash Type of weaving where the wrap threads are wrapped with the weft to make the pattern.

Nahiyah District or region; refers to the settled areas of northern Jordan who formed defense regions to repel Bedouin raids.

Nay End-blown flute made of reed or metal.

Qadud al-Halabiyyah A type of music based on the *muwashshahah* developed in Aleppo.

Qa'id Commander or leader; in Jordan the term was applied to the person selected to serve as the military leader in case of Bedouin attack.

Qanun Term has a number of applications; law; type of plucked zither used in classical Arabic music; small clay or metal brazier found in rural homes.

Qasidah Long poem.

Qiyas Analogy; one of the five major sources for Islamic law.

Qumbaz Man's overcoat worn over the dishdashah; often made of heavier types of cloth and made to be tied at the shoulder and waist.

Rabab One stringed bowed instrument often used to accompany recitations of poetry.

Rabab al-Sha'ir The Poet's Rabab.

Ragm Type of weaving where the design is made by using different colored warp threads that are exposed by the weft otherwise left to "float" along the back of the piece.

Raqs Dance; raqs baladi and raqs sharqi refer to belly dance.

Riqq Tambourine.

Ru'a Designation for those Bedouin who have traditionally been semi-settled and whose migration patterns were very limited. They raised small stock such as sheep and goats and raised some agricultural products such as wheat or maintained small orchards of fruit trees.

Rubi'at Short poem composed in four lines.

Ruffah Sides of tent.

Ruwaq Back wall of a tent.

Safalah Lower part of the back of the tent that touches the ground.

Sahah Tent divider to separate the private, family side of the tent from the public, men's side.

Salah(t) Prayer; in Islam there are five daily prayers.

Sanjaq Turkish term for a flag and during the Ottoman period applied to the smallest level of administrative district.

Saz Turkish ancestor of the buzuk; a long necked lute with metal strings with the lower register used as a drone when played, which gives a distinctive sound to Turkish music.

Shabriyyah   Traditional dagger worn by Bedouin men.

Shagag   Roof pieces of the tent.

Shahadah   Declaration of faith "There is no god but God and Muhammad is the Prophet of God."

Shambar   Light cloth worn traditionally by women to cover their hair, face, and neck.

Shari'ah   Islamic law.

Sharif   Term used to designate direct descendants of the Prophet Muhammad.

Shawayah   Designation for those Bedouin tribes who have traditionally raised small stock such as sheep and goats, which limits their migration range.

Shi'a (Shi'i)   From the Arabic phrase Shi'at 'Ali, or the Partisans of 'Ali, who were the supporters of 'Ali ibn Talib, cousin and son in law of the Prophet Muhammad, in his bid to be the head of the Islamic state.

Shimagh   Traditional head cloth worn by men; the shimagh is of high quality usually being a mix of cotton and silk.

Shrak or Marquq   Type of wafer thin bread popular with the Bedouin.

Simsimiyah   A lyre; ancient musical instrument still played by some Bedouin in the region.

Sirwal   Turkish trousers; the wide, baggy traditional trousers worn by men in the region.

Sitar   Front of a tent brought down to indicate no one is home or the family is not prepared to receive guests.

Siyam   Fast during the month of Ramadan.

Sufi   Islamic mystic.

Suhur   Last meal of the night before the day's fast begins during Ramadan.

Sultan   Ruler; literally the person who holds real temporal power and authority.

Sunnah   The actions of the Prophet Muhammad; one of the five major sources for Islamic law.

Sunni   From the Arabic phrase Ahl al-Sunnah or People who abide by the Practice of the Prophet. They supported the succession of the Prophet through election by a consultative council rather than the blood descent from 'Ali.

Suq   Market.

Surah   Chapter of the Qu'ran.

Tabun   Oven.

Tar   Large, round single-headed drum with a wooden frame.

Tarawih   Extra prayer offered during Ramadan after the 'Ishiyah prayer.

Tarbush   Turkish term for the red felt conical hat worn by Ottoman officials and urban men in the late Ottoman period.

Thob   Clothes; dress.

Thob 'Ob (Khalagah)   Large double-dress common among Bedouin women and some Jordanian village women. The dress was so large that it was pulled up over a belt causing heavy folds to fall back down to the woman's ankles.

'Ud   Arabic ancestor to the European lute. Oval-shaped string instrument played with a feather plectrum. Its soft, deep sounds makes it the "king" of Arabic instruments and a favorite for solo performances.

Umm Arabic for mother; used as an honorific title such as Umm Muhammad or Mother of Muhammad to note the eldest male child of the family.

Wadi Valley or small, seasonal stream.

Wasat Middle; in a tent refers to the main middle pole.

Wazir Government minister; *wizarah* is a government ministry.

Wudu' Ablution; ritual washing required of all Muslims prior to prayer.

Ya Hala' Welcome; a shortened version of "Ahlan" often used in phrases such as "Ya Hala' bil-Dayf" (or "Welcome to our guest").

Zajal Type of poem easily adapted to music.

Zakat Poor tax; money collected from those who can afford it at the end of Ramadan to be given to the poor.

Bibliography

Abidi, Aqil. *Jordan: A Political Study.* London: Asia Publishing House, 1965.

Abu Jaber, Kamil. *The Jordanians and the People of Jordan.* Amman: Royal Scientific Society, 1980.

Abu Jaber, Kamil and Fawzi Gharaibeh. "Bedouin Settlement: Organizational, Legal, and Administrative Stucture in Jordan." In *The Future of Pastoral Peoples,* eds. J Galaty, P. Salzman, and D. Araonson, 294–300. Ottowa: International Development Research Center, 1981.

Abu-Lughod, Lila. *Veiled Sentiments: Honor and Poetry in a Bedouin Society.* Cairo: The American University in Cairo Press, 1986.

Amiry, Suad and Vera Tamari. *The Palestinian Village Home.* London: British Museum Publication, 1989.

Antoun, Richard. *Arab Village: A Social Structural Study of a Trans-Jordanian Peasant Community.* Bloomington: Indiana University Press, 1972.

Aruri, Nasser. *Jordan: A Study in Politics.* The Hague: Martinus Nijhoff, 1972.

Bacharach, Jere. *A Near Eastern Studies Handbook.* Seattle: University of Washington Press, 1976.

Badawi, M. *Modern Arabic Literature.* Cambridge: Cambridge University Press, 1993.

Badr, Liyana. *A Balcony over the Fakihani.* Translated by Peter Clark and Christopher Tingley. New York: Interlink Books, 2002.

Beaumaont, Peter, Gerald Blake, and Malcom Wagstaff. *The Middle East.* London: John Wiley and Sons, 1976.

Bourbon, Fabio. *Petra Jordan's Extraordinary Ancient City.* New York: Barnes and Noble Books, 2004.

Chatty, Dawn. *From Camel to Truck: The Bedouin in the Modern World.* New York: Vantage Press, 1986.

Cleveland, William. *A History of the Modern Middle East.* Boulder, CO: Westview Press, 1994.

Creswell, K.A.C. *A Short Account of Early Muslim Architecture.* Cairo: The American University in Cairo Press, 1989.

Dallas, R. *King Hussein: A Life on the Edge.* London: Profile Books, 1998.

Faqir, Fadia. *Pillars of Salt.* New York: Interlink Books, 2004.

Fisher, W. B. *The Middle East: A Physical, Social, and Regional Geography.* London: Methuen and Company, Ltd, 1971.

Fernea, Elizabeth and Basima Bezirgan, eds. *Middle Eastern Muslim Women Speak.* Austin: University of Texas Press, 1977.

Fernea, Elizabeth Warnock, ed. *Women and the Family in the Middle East: New Voices of Change.* Austin: University of Texas Press, 1984.

Glubb, John Bagot. *A Soldier with the Arabs.* London: Hodder and Stoughton, 1957.

———. *Syria, Lebanon, and Jordan.* New York: Walker and Company, 1967.

Gubser, Peter. *Jordan: Crossroads of Middle Eastern Events.* Boulder, CO: Westview Press, 1983.

Hafez, Sabry and Catherine Cobban, eds. *A Reader of Modern Arabic Short Stories.* London: Al Saqi Books, 1988.

Harding, G. Lankaster. *The Antiquities of Jordan.* London: James Clarke and Company, Ltd, 1967.

Hiatt, Joseph. "State Formation and Encapsulation of Nomads: Local Change and Continuity Among Recently Sedentarized Bedouin in Jordan." *Nomadic Peoples* 15 (1984): 1–11.

Hitti, Philip. *History of the Arabs.* London: St. Martin's Press, 1973.

Hussein of Jordan, King. *Uneasy Lies the Head: An Autobiography of King Hussein of Jordan.* London: Heinemann, 1962.

Jayyusi, Salma Khadra. *Modern Arabic Poetry.* New York: Columbia University Press, 1991.

Johnson-Davies, Denys, selected and translated by. *Under the Naked Sky: Short Stories from the Arab World.* New York: The American University in Cairo Press, 2003.

Jureidini, Paul and R.D. McLaurin. *Jordan: Impact of the Social Change on the Role of the Tribes.* New York: Praeger, 1984.

Kalter, Johannes, ed. *The Arts and Crafts of Syria.* London: Thames and Hudson Ltd, 1992.

Kawar, Widad, Marian Awwad, and Maria Abu Risha. *Weaving in Jordan.* Amman: The Jordan Crafts Council, 1980.

Khalifeh, Sahar. *Wild Thorns.* Translated by Trevor LeGassick and Elizabeth Fernea. London: Al Saqi Books, 1985.

Khouri, Rami. *Petra: A Brief Guide to the Antiquities.* Amman: Al Kutba Publications, 1989.

Lancaster, William. *The Rwala Bedouin Today,* 2nd ed. Prospect Heights, IL: Waveland Press, Inc., 1981.

Layne, Linda. *Home and Homeland: The Dialogics of Tribal and National Identities in Jordan.* Princeton: Princeton University Press, 1994.

Lewis, Bernard, ed. *The World of Islam: Faith, People, Culture.* London: Thames and Hudson, 1976.

Lewis, Norman. *Nomads and Settlers in Syria and Jordan, 1800–1900.* New York: Cambridge University Press, 1987.

Lias, Godfrey. *Glubb's Legion.* London: Evans Bros., Ltd, 1956.

Lunt, James. *Hussein of Jordan: A Political Biography.* London: Macmillan, 1989.

Ma'oz, Moshe. *Ottoman Reforms in Syria and Palestine 1840–1861.* London: Oxford University Press, 1970.

Munif, Abd al-Rahman. *Story of a City: Childhood in Amman.* Translated by Samira Kawar. London: Quartet Books, 1998.

Musil, Alois. *The Manners and Customs of the Ru'ala Bedouins.* New York: Charles R. Crane, 1928.

Nasrallah, Ibrahim. *Prairies of Fever.* Translated by May Jayyusi and Jeremy Reed. New York: Interlink Books, 1993.

Nicholson, R.A. *Literary History of the Arabs.* Cambridge: University of Cambridge Press, 1969.

Nyrop, Richard. *Jordan, a Country Study.* Washington, DC: American University, 1980.

Ochsenwald, William. *The Hijaz Railway.* Charlottesville: University of Virginia Press, 1980.

Pappe, Ilan. *A Modern History of Palestine: One Land, Two People.* Cambridge: Cambridge University Press, 2004.

Patai, Raphael. *The Kingdom of Jordan.* Princeton, NJ: Princeton University Press, 1958.

Peake, Ferderick. *History and Tribes of Jordan.* Coral Gables, FL: University of Miami Press, 1958.

Plascow, Avi. *The Palestinian Refugees in Jordan, 1948–1957.* London: Cass, 1981.

Provence, Michael. *The Great Syrian Revolt and the Rise of Arab Nationalism.* Austin: University of Texas Press, 2005

Racy, A. J. *Making Music in the Arab World : The Culture and Artistry of Tarab.* Cambridge: Cambridge University Press, 2003.

Rajab, Jehan. *Palestinian Costume.* New York: Kegan Paul International, 1989.

Raswan, Carl. *Black Tents of Arabia (My Life Among the Bedouin).* Boston: Little, Brown and Company, 1935.

Robins, Philip. *A History of Jordan.* Cambridge: Cambridge University Press, 2004.

Rollin, Sue and Jane Streetly. *Blue Guide: Jordan.* New York: A & C Black, 2001.

Rogan, Eugene and Tariq Tell, eds. *Village, Steppe and State: The Social Origins of Modern Jordan.* London: British Academic Press, 1994.

Sabbagh, Suha, ed. *Arab Women: Between Defiance and Restraint.* New York: Olive Branch Press, 1996.

Salibi, Kamal. *The Modern History of Jordan.* London: IB Tauris, 1993.

Shoup, John. *The Bedouins of Jordan: History and Sedentarization.* MA thesis, University of Utah, 1980.

———. "Pastoral Nomadism in Jordan and Syria." *Cultural Survival Quarterly* 8(1) (1984):11–15.

———. "Impact of Tourism on the Bedouin of Petra, Jordan." *The Middle East Journal* 39(2) (1985): 277–291.

———. *Hima: A Traditional Bedouin Land-Use System in Contemporary Syria and Jordan.* PhD diss., Washington University in St. Louis, 1990.

Shryock, Andrew. *Nationalism and the Genealogical Imagination: Oral History and Textual Authority in Tribal Jordan.* Berkeley: University of California Press, 1997.

Shwadran, Benjamin. *Jordan, a State of Tension.* New York: Council for Middle Eastern Affairs Press, 1959.

Snow, Peter. *Hussein: A Biography.* Washington, DC: R.B. Luce, 1972.

Vatikiotis, P.J. *Politics and the Military in Jordan: A Study of the Arab Legion, 1921–1967.* London: Cass, 1967.

Weir, Shelagh. *The Bedouin.* London: British Museum Publication, 1990.

Weir, Shelagh and Serene Shahid. *Palestinian Embroidery.* London: British Museum Publication, 1988.

Wilson, Rodney, ed. *Politics and the Economy in Jordan.* London: Routledge, 1991.

Zeine, Zeine. *The Struggle for Arab Independence.* Delmar, NY: Caravan Books, 1977.

Zubaida, Sami and Richard Tapper, eds. *A Taste of Thyme: Culinary Cultures of the Middle East.* New York: Taurus Parke Paperbacks, 2000.

Index

About the Author

JOHN A. SHOUP is Associate Professor of anthropology at Al Akhawayn University in Ifrane, Morocco.